May God add His blessings
as you enjoy His Word
through these rhymes!

Gene Crumbley Rom 10:9

BIBLE *Stories*
IN RHYME
and other Poems

Presented to:

_____

By:

_____

Date:

_____

Occasion:

_____

_____

_____

Bible Stories in Rhyme and Other Poems
0-88144-288-7
Copyright © 2007 by Dr. G. E. Crumbley, Sr.

Cover: Church photo taken by the Author.
Crescent Hill Baptist Church
Nacoochee Road
Helen, GA

This little mountain church is built very much like the one attended by the author as a youth, and in which he first heard many of the Bible stories in this book.

Dedication

Introduction

One night while reading the story of David and Goliath, the Lord laid it on my heart to use the talent He had given me to put the story to rhyme. I did just that, and the next thing I know He is leading me through His Word putting other famous, and not so famous, stories to rhyme. After doing several of them such as Adam and Eve, Jonah and the Whale and Noah and the Ark, I read them to my dear wife who encouraged me to put them into book form. Each time I thought I was finished, the Lord showed me another one to do. Some other poems and song lyrics I had written over the years were added, and thus this book "Bible Stories in Rhyme" was created.

It is my hope and desire that as you read these poems you will be inspired, encouraged, and drawn closer to God. These stories are easy to read in verse form and easy to remember, so you will be able to apply their principles to everyday life. Many people find them to be very well suited for use as devotionals in Church, Sunday School, and Christian gatherings.

If you are reading this book and have never accepted Jesus Christ as your Lord and Saviour, it is my prayer that the Lord will touch your heart through these poems in such a way that you will become aware of your need for Him in your life. The Bible tells us that it is only through His sinless blood that we can enter the Kingdom of Heaven.

May God bless you, as you read His Word through these stories and poems, as much He did me as I wrote them.

The Author

BIBLE *Stories* IN RHYME

and other Poems

Inspiring

Encouraging

Enlightening

and well suited for *Devotionals*

Dr. Gene Crumbley

God created the earth
And looked down with a smile
And must have said this is good
This is really worthwhile.
He made all the creatures,
Including the dove,
And enjoyed each of them
From His Home, up above.
But something was missing
In this His great plan,
That something was a human
Whom He would call Man.
So He reached down and took
Some dust from the earth
And molded and shaped it,
And then gave Adam birth.
God was so pleased
It was now His opinion
Adam could rule
So He gave him dominion,
Over all the creatures
Whom he could now name,
Adam thought this was fun
It was just like a game.
But God saw that Adam
Was lonely down there
And needed a partner
With whom he could share,

All his innermost feelings
And the things that he had
And have someone to hold
So he wouldn't feel sad.
God put Adam to sleep
And took out a rib bone
And created a woman
So he wouldn't be alone.
They enjoyed the garden
And all of its bliss
And thought that it always
Would be just like this.
But along came old Satan
That snake of deceit,
Who tempted poor Eve
And her will did defeat,
With his cunning sly wit
When he told her that lie,
If you eat of that tree,
You won't surely die!
Without even thinking
Of what would be her fate,
She took some of the fruit
And then quickly ate,
From the tree of knowledge
Which she should have let be,
For she knew good from evil
As God did, you see.
Then Adam ate too
Knowing it was not right
And his eyes were opened
And with this new insight,

They saw they were naked
And they now understood
Those things that were evil,
From those that were good.
They got some fig leaves
Their bodies to cover
For they were ashamed
When they looked at each other.
They heard God in the garden
And ran away to hide.
When He asked, where are you?
They kept their responses inside.
They couldn't face God
For they were sorely afraid
So they hid in some bushes
Way back in the shade.
God then asked those two
Why did you eat of the tree!
Adam blamed the woman,
Saying, she enticed me.
Eve blamed the serpent
It was his fault she ate,
She knew she shouldn't have,
But it was now too late.
God destined the serpent
To be cursed more than all
And for the rest of his life
On his belly, he'd crawl.
To woman God promised
To multiply her sorrow
With great pain on childbirth
This much to her horror!

And for Adam because
He also ate from the tree,
The ground was now cursed
And forever would be.
From dust you were made
And to dust you'll return,
This saying from God
Caused Adam concern.
God then made some clothing
Out of animal skin,
To clothe Adam and Eve
And because of their sin,
Cast them out of the garden
But they didn't know yet,
They'd live a life full of misery
With tears, toil and sweat.
Now all of this happened
Because God wasn't obeyed,
If those two had done that
Today we'd all have it made!

Romans 5:9

For by one man's disobedience many were made sinners;
so by the obedience of one shall many be made righteous.

Romans 6:10

For in that He died unto sin once; but in that He liveth,
He liveth unto God.

God appeared to Solomon
In a dream one night
And asked, what shall I give you?
This was Solomon's plight.
He said, Lord you've made me king
Over these whose number is great,
I need to know how to rule them
For I now control their fate.
God really loved Solomon
And this pleased Him so much,
For he asked only for wisdom,
And not for riches, gold and such.
God then gave him wisdom
And an understanding heart,
With the ability to see good and evil
And tell the two apart.
Two women came before him
With a story so very wild
And had a baby with them,
Each claiming it was her child.
It seems they both had given birth,
But one mother's baby died
And she stole the other mother's baby,
And put her dead one by her side.
My baby was alive last night,
Is what one mother said
But when I woke up this morning
A dead child was there instead.

Not so! Said the other woman,
And each one stood by her story.
Then the decision Solomon made
Brought him fame and glory.
He sent for a very sharp sword
And said, I'll cut this child in two,
Then once that is done
I'll give a half to each of you.
One woman said, Divide the child,
Let it be neither hers nor mine,
But the other one said, don't do it!
Give it to her and that will be fine.
Solomon gave the child to the woman,
Who from it was willing to part,
For he knew she was the mother
And loved that baby with all her heart.

Christmas Candles

Christmas candles give off such a warm glow
At this special season that Christians love so,
When our Lord and Saviour, Jesus Christ, was born
On the day we know as Christmas morn.
Eternal life is the planned destiny
That God has designed for you and me.
That's why He gave us His only Son
And was very pleased with what He had done.
Jesus was born, that He later may die
To provide a way to eternity, for both you and I.

Jonah and the Whale

There was a city called Nineveh
That had drawn God's great ire,
Because it was full of wickedness,
Just filled with muck and mire.
So God sent word to Jonah,
Go tell them to change their ways
Or I will destroy their city,
And I'll give them just forty days.
But Jonah went down to Joppa
Which was the opposite way
And got on a ship to Tarshish,
He would sure regret that day.
For God caused a storm to come
And the ship was tossed about.
The men on board were so afraid,
Even the very strong and stout.
So each man prayed to his god
To seek a reason for this storm,
Every man except Jonah, that is,
Who was sleeping nice and warm,
The shipmaster then awoke him
To see if he might just know why
They were caught up in these angry seas,
But Jonah told this man a lie.
He said he didn't know anything,
When all the time he knew,
He was keeping the truth to himself
For fear of what they'd do.

The men decided to cast lots
To see which man was at fault
And causing all these mighty waves
And try to bring them to a halt.

Each man then cast his lot
And the lots fell right on Jonah.
Now he had to tell the truth
Even though he didn't "wan'na".

He told them he was a Hebrew
Whose God made sea and land
And who had given him a job to do,
But that he had turned and ran.

They asked Jonah what they should do
And he said, throw me overboard,
I am the reason for this storm
And that will appease my Lord.

These men didn't want to do this,
But did just as Jonah said,
Afraid if they did not do it
They all would end up dead.

As they threw him overboard
God chose a way to save his soul,
By sending a great big fish
To swallow Jonah whole.

Jonah spent three days and nights
In the belly of that whale,
And he was so afraid in there
His skin became very pale.

But Jonah learned his lesson
And now needed nothing more,
So God caused the whale to vomit
And Jonah ended up on the shore.

He promised God he would obey
Each and every new command
And went straight down to Nineveh,
That wicked, sinful land.
He told all the people there
About his great God Jehovah
Who would soon destroy their city,
That is how he won them over.
They now believed in his God
And they all began to fast.
Even the king came off his throne
And put on sackcloth and ash.
When God saw how they had changed,
In His own heart He relented
And did not do as once planned
For these people had repented.
Thousands were saved because Jonah,
Did finally listen and obey,
Which is what we, ourselves must do
And not turn and run away,
But tell everyone about Jesus
Who gave His life for all, you see,
When He hung upon that old rugged cross
And shed His blood at Calvary.

1 Samuel 15:

22b.   *Behold, to obey is better than sacrifice.*

23a.   *For rebellion is as the sin of witchcraft,*
         and stubbornness is as iniquity and idolatry.

My Friend

I have a good friend that I want you to meet,
He is the one who makes my life complete.
He's always there with me through thick and thin
And never leaves me, even when I sin.
He'll never forsake me during bad times in life
Such as sickness and sorrow and troubles and strife.
I can call upon Him whether daytime or night
And He is always there to help make things right.
He never judges me, which in this world is rare,
But continues to love me with such tender care.
I'd like you to meet Him, this dear trusted friend,
For I know once you do He'll be yours till the end.
A true friend is one who is determined and bound
To love and protect you, even lay his life down.
My friend did that when He hung on that cross,
His name is Jesus, and without Him, we're lost!

As the old Hymn says:
"What a friend we have in Jesus"

You could hear the steel swords
And the brass armor rattle
As the Philistines gathered
Their army for battle,
On the side of a mountain
Overlooking a valley,
Waiting for King Saul
And his army to rally.
Then out of their camp
Came a giant of a man,
His name was Goliath
And he took his stand.
He cast a great shadow
For he was ten feet tall,
And he cried out in scorn
To the camp of King Saul.
Why come with your army
To set this battle array,
Just choose you one man
To fight me this day.
If he can defeat me
Then you'll remain free
And each one of us
Your servants will be.
But should I prevail
And spill his blood in the dust,
You and your people
Will be servants for us!
When Saul heard these words
He was truly dismayed
For each man in his army
Was sorely afraid.

The giant taunted Israel
For forty days straight.
Saul had no one to fight him
So his fear became great.
Just when it seemed
Things were about to get messy,
Along came young David
The brave son of Jesse.
He was sent by his father
To take his brothers some food,
But when he got there
They were in a sad mood.
They were headed for battle
And feared that they might
Be wounded or killed
In the oncoming fight.
Goliath challenged again,
This time David heard
And as Saul's army trembled,
He said, This is absurd!
Who is this Philistine
That he should defy,
The armies of our living God;
This heathen must die!
David's brother heard this
And with anger like fire
He criticized David
Till it pricked like a briar.
The king heard about David
And sent for this man,
He said, I have no one to fight him
Do you think you can?
Yes! Replied David,
Don't let your heart fail,
I'll go down in that valley,
Down in that vale,

For your servant did slay
Both a lion and a bear
And saved all the sheep
That were put in his care.
God delivered me then
And with this Philistine
He will do it again
Though this giant is so mean,
But he has defied God
And he'll surely regret it,
I'll take him down in a way
So no one will forget it!
But to Saul, David's chances
Looked mighty slim
For all the king's armor
Was too heavy for him.
He couldn't wear the helmet
Or carry the sword,
But said, I'll do this battle
For you and my Lord.
His staff and his sling
Was all that he took
And in the valley he chose
Five stones from a brook.
He only needed one
But he took the four others,
For he heard the giant
May have four brothers.
When the giant saw that David
Was just a mere lad
He was filled with contempt
And became very mad.
He said to small David,
Come hither to me
And then when I slay you
Saul's army will flee.

David said to Goliath,
With fright you should quiver
For into my hands this day,
Will my God deliver,
You whom I'll smite
And then cut off your head,
And we'll slay all your army
Once you are dead.
This battle is God's
So the whole world will know
There's a great God in Israel
Who loves them so.
As the Philistine arose
And began to draw nigh
David swiftly ran toward him
And let the stone fly.
The stone smote Goliath
And sunk in like lead,
When he fell to the ground,
David cut off his head.
The Philistine army
Could not believe their eyes,
How such a small lad
Cut this giant down to his size.
When the soldiers now saw
That their champion was slain
They attempted to flee
But their flight was in vain,
For Saul's army chased them
And slew every man.
This happened because a young boy,
Said, With God's help I can!

(When we face the Goliaths, (troubles) in our lives, we must trust God for our deliverance just as David did.)

The loss of a Christian loved one
Is always so hard to bear
But they're now with Christ in Heaven
And someday we'll see them there.
For that is God's promise to us
In His precious Holy Word,
That absence from this body
Means presence with the Lord.
Yes, there will be grief and sorrow
But God will see us through the pain,
As we realize that our loss
Is really Heaven's gain.
So may God's closeness comfort us
In those sorrowful days ahead,
And may His Word give us strength
Just like our daily bread.

2 Corinthians 5:

6b.   *while we are at home in the body, we are absent from the Lord:*

8.   *We are confident, I say, and willing rather to be absent from the body, and present with the Lord.*

Samson and Delilah

Samson was a very strong man
But he must have been real dense,
For Delilah tricked him so many times
That it didn't make much sense.
It all started when he fell in love,
And they say that love is blind,
But in his case it was more than that;
It must have numbed his mind.
This pretty woman that he loved
Down in the valley of Sorek,
Was offered money to betray him
But poor Samson did not suspect.
She collected from each Philistine
Eleven hundred silver coins,
And Samson would soon regret
The very day that he was born.
One day Delilah said to him,
Wherein does your strength lie
That I may bind and afflict you?
This was her very first try.
He said, Bind me with seven vines
Ones that never have been dried
And I could not break loose
No matter how hard I tried.
So she bound him with the vines
With the Philistines lying in wait,
Then said, your enemies are upon you
And he broke them with strength so great.

She said, you have teased and mocked me
And told me lies so now I pray,
Tell me how you may be bound
So you cannot get away.

Samson told her a second time,
Take new ropes and bind me fast
And I will be weak like any man
And can then be caught at last.

So Delilah took new ropes
And while he slept that night
Wrapped them around Samson
Making sure they were tight.

After doing this she told him
The Philistines are at your bed.
He woke up and broke the ropes
As if they were only thread.

The third time she did as told
And tied his hair to the bed with a pin,
Then suddenly woke him up
But he got away again.

Now Delilah pressed him daily,
Today we'd call that nagging,
And Samson finally told her the truth,
It was as if he was bragging.

He said his hair had never been cut
From the day that he was born,
And he would lose all his strength
If his hair was ever shorn.

So while he lay there sleeping
She had a man shave his head,
And he awoke thinking he was strong
But he was very weak instead.

He had given away his secret
And his Lord had now departed.
His enemies afflicted him greatly;
How that must have smarted.
They put out both his eyes
And made him grind in the prison house,
So the once mighty Samson
Was as meek as a tiny mouse.
But God answered Samson's last prayer
For his afflictions to avenge,
And gave Samson all his strength back
So he could get his full revenge.
The people were all making merry
By drinking wine and eating, we know,
And having Samson make sport for them,
And he was putting on quite a good "show".
He then pushed against the pillars
That were so tall and round,
And the temple fell killing everyone.
He literally, "Brought the house down".
Now this event was brought about
By a woman who wasn't his wife,
But those he killed at his own death
Were more than he killed all his life.
We Christians are sometimes like Samson,
Although he was really one of a kind.
At times we're like that old saying,
We have a "strong back, but a weak mind".

Isaiah 12:12b

Behold the Lord Jehovah is my strength and my song;
He also is become my salvation

In the days of a king named Darius
There was a wise, trustworthy man.
His name was Daniel and he was wiser,
Than anyone else in the land.
The king granted him much power
And all the people knew his name.
He had power over all the king's men
And continued to grow in fame.
This made the other men jealous
Because they had to answer to him
And their chance of getting more power
Was getting even more slim.
These men plotted against Daniel
But he was loyal, steadfast and true.
They couldn't find any fault in him
So they didn't know what to do.
But they knew he loved God deeply
And not once but three times a day
Got in front of an open window
And knelt down on his knees to pray.
They worked on the king's prideful nature
And got him to sign a decree,
Bringing death to all in the kingdom
Who worshipped any god other than he.
This decree would last thirty days
And according to the law of the land
Could not be changed by anyone,
Not even the king's own hand.
As soon as the king signed the order,
These men all smiled and said,
Daniel bows down to his own God
And must be punished until he is dead.

The king sent his most trusted servants
To bring his friend Daniel in haste,
For he knew what he had to do,
Though it would be a terrible waste.
They threw Daniel into the lions' den
And blocked the entrance with a stone,
Then left him there for those hungry lions
To eat the flesh off all his bones.
The king went back to his chambers
But couldn't get Daniel out of his mind
Because he really loved this man
Who was good and wise and kind.
The king arose very early
And could hardly wait to begin
Making his way through the castle
And down to the lions' den.
He got close and cried out with feeling
Daniel are you alive down there?
He waited anxiously for an answer
And finally heard Daniel declare,
O king, now live forever,
My God shut the lions' jaws
For I have done no hurt to you
And have broken none of God's laws.
So Daniel was pulled from the lions' den
With no bites on his body or neck
His accusers were thrown into the pit
And not one did the lions reject.
Now Daniel's steadfast belief in God
Was really what pulled him through
And it was so obvious to everyone,
Now even the king believed in Him too!
If we, when in trouble, trust in God
Like Daniel in that lions' den,
Those around us may be drawn to God
And accept Jesus as Saviour and Friend.

One day God looked down on the earth
And saw that it was now evil and corrupt
And decided to destroy everything
But the destruction would not be abrupt.
For Noah found grace in the eyes of God,
And God told him to build an ark,
He had no idea what that could be
But was to make it of wood without bark.
It was to be four hundred fifty feet long
And some seventy five feet wide,
Forty five feet high and three stories tall
With a window above and a door on the side.
God said, When it is done I'll send a flood
And everything on the earth will die,
But all your family will be safe in the ark
Out of the rain coming down, from the sky.
You will put two creatures of every sort
Into the ark where they'll survive,
Male and female of each living thing
And you will keep them all alive.
So take all the food you will need
To feed them, and your family.
Noah did as God commanded,
Yes, everything God told him did he.
God then told Noah to get in the ark
With his family of each generation
For he alone was found righteous,
That's the reason for his Salvation.

God then closed the door of the ark
And steady rains did then begin
And Noah couldn't open the door
So no one else could get in.

The waters rose above the trees
And the hills and mountains high,
So everything that moved on earth,
Would not live but would surely die.

The amount of water covering the earth
Was so vast it would truly amaze,
And lasted so long and did not subside
For one hundred and fifty days.

The raven went forth and came back again,
Which meant water still covered the ground.
A dove was sent once, and then again
Coming back with a leaf it had found.

The ark was resting on Mount Ararat
So God told Noah it's time to leave
And to also take the animals off
I am sure Noah was quite relieved.

Now God blessed the family of Noah
And told him the earth to replenish,
By being fruitful and multiplying
And He would be with them till the finish.

Now with all that wickedness on the earth
The righteousness of one man shone through,
Which says one man can make a difference,
Could that one man be you?

2 Corinthians 5:21
For He hath made Him (Jesus) to be sin for us, who knew no sin;
*that we may be made the **righteousness** of God in Him.*

God called out to Abraham
Who answered, here am I,
And God said, Take your son Isaac
To a place where he must die.
Now Abraham loved God so much
He followed this strange command
And did not question God at all
Though he did not understand.
They traveled to that far place,
To that mountain called Moriah,
Taking the wood they would need
To build a great big fire
Isaac called out to his father
Who replied, Son here I am.
Isaac said, Father, we have fire and wood,
But we do not have a lamb.
Abraham told him not to worry,
For he was trusting God inside,
And knew within his heart,
A lamb God would provide.
Then Isaac was bound up tightly
And laid on that pile of wood,
It looked real bad for Isaac now
But it would surely turn out good.
As Abraham raised his hand
That held that long sharp knife
An angel spoke to him saying,
Do not take your son's life.

For God now knows you fear Him,
You have proven it this day,
There's a ram over in the thicket
That's the one you must slay.
Now God knew Abraham was willing
To sacrifice his only son,
This must be a picture of God
Because it's exactly what He has done.
He put His only Son on the cross,
Letting Him die there for our sin
And for all who accept His sacrifice,
A brand new life will then begin.

John 3:16

For God so loved the world that He gave
His only begotten Son, that whosoever believes in Him
should not perish, but have everlasting life.

Hebrews 11:6

But without faith it is impossible to please Him:
for he that comes to God must first believe
He is, and that He is a rewarder of them that
that diligently seek Him.

The children of Israel did evil again,
Once more in the sight of the Lord,
So He sold them to the Canaanites
And they would now live under the sword,
Of the Canaanite captain Sisera
Who had nine hundred chariots of iron,
And who oppressed them for twenty years,
He was mighty like a lion.
Now Deborah was a lady Judge
Who dwelt under a big palm tree,
And the Israelites were judged by her
And she was as fair as she could be.
The Lord promised to free Israel
If she sent Barak with an army strong,
But he refused to go without her
And what he did was very wrong.
So Deborah agreed to go with him
To help him set these people free,
But told him the honor and glory
Would go to a woman and not he.
She then lured Sisera's army
As promised down to the river,
Where Barak slew many men
But Sisera she did not deliver.
He got down off his chariot,
And getting away was his intent,
But he made a fatal mistake
When he went in Jael's tent.

He was very tired and thirsty,
So she gave him some milk to drink.
That warm milk made him so sleepy,
He fell asleep quick as a wink.
Now Jael was a smart woman
And her plan for Sisera was simple,
While he slept she took a tent stake
And drove it through his temple.
She then went out and told Barak
In my tent is the man you seek,
So God delivered Sisera not to him
But to this woman so mild and meek.
The children of Israel prospered
And God met their every need.
He let women do a man's job,
These two were a special breed.
So listen up men this tells us,
When God gives us a job to do,
We must step right up and take control
And not fail to follow through.

1 Corinthians 16:13

*Be alert and on your guard; stand firm in your faith,
act like men and be courageous; grow in strength.*

Eagle's Landing Baptist Folks

(sung to the tune of "Shoo Fly Pie and Apple Pan Dowdy».)

Eagle's Landing Baptist folks and Pastor Tim Dowdy
They set your hearts on fire for they always say howdy.
They always smile as they greet you with a big handshake
And they teach you God's Word for so much is at stake.
Now if you don't know Jesus you can sure find Him here,
All you have to do is listen, just open up an ear,
And you'll learn all about him and His abiding love
And how you can spend eternity in Heaven above.

Keep on preaching God's word, Pastor Tim Dowdy.
We never get enough of that wonderful stuff!

Now before your life is over and come to an end
Won't you please accept Jesus, He'll take away your sin
With the blood that He shed on that cross at Calvary
And from that day on a new creature you'll be.

Pastor, when you preach,
Pastor, every soul you reach,
For our God so ever-loving,
You'll save from Satan's red hot oven!
Keep on preaching God's Word Pastor Tim Dowdy,
We never get enough of that wonderful stuff.

(When my wife and I first visited Eagle's Landing First Baptist Church we were very impressed with their friendliness and the pastor's dedication to preaching God's Word, hence these lyrics were written.)

A centurion heard about Jesus
And how He could heal the sick
And sent Jewish elders to find Him
And ask Him to come real quick.

This man had a good reputation
So Jesus decided to go by
And help this man's dear servant
Who was sick and about to die.

When Jesus was not far away
And would soon be under his roof,
The man sent word he was not worthy
And Jesus knew that this was proof,

That the centurion believed in Him
And that his faith was very real
For he said, Just say the word
And my servant will be healed.

I too, am a man under authority
And many servants I command,
And when I say do this or that
They do it each and every man.

When Christ heard these words
He truly marveled at this man,
Who knew He had the power to heal
Without even lifting His hand.

Jesus said to those around Him,
Such great faith I've not found
In all the land of Israel,
This man's faith is really sound!

The Lame Man Healed

Peter and John went to the temple
One day at the hour of prayer
And once they had arrived,
Saw a lame man lying there.
He was at the gate called Beautiful
Asking for alms as people went in.
He was lame from his birth
And not because of any sin.
He sought money from Peter
Who said, Silver or gold have I none,
But such as I have I will give you
And you can thank God when it's done.
The fact that you are lame
Is not really your own fault,
So in the name of Jesus Christ,
You can now get up and walk.
This man leaped up and stood
And entered the temple with them,
Walking, leaping and praising God,
And maybe even singing a Hymn.
People asked how they could heal
But Peter said, It's not us,
God Himself healed this man
To glorify His Son Jesus.
Peter and John preached to these people
That Jesus died, was buried and arose
And many who heard their words believed,
To be exact, five thousand of those.

Jesus Knows Me This I Love
(sung to tune of Jesus Loves Me)

Jesus knows me this I love
As He looks down from above,
Knows my life from inside out
Tries to bring a change about.

Yes, Jesus **knows** me,
Yes, Jesus **knows** me,
Yet, Jesus loves me,
He tells me in His Word.

He not only knows my name,
But He knows my mind and frame.
Knows each hair upon my head;
Knows the kind of life I've led.

(chorus)
Don't you know He knows you too,
Every thought and deed you do.
He will surely lead your way
If you trust Him every day

Yes, Jesus **knows** me,
Yes, Jesus **knows** me,
Yet, Jesus loves me,
He tells me in His Word.

(These lyrics were inspired by a message with the same title
preached at First Baptist Church, Atlanta by Rev. Jack R. Taylor.)

The Prodigal Son

A certain man had two sons
And the youngest of them pled,
Father give me my inheritance
And it was done just as he said.
Not many days thereafter,
He gathered his goods to himself,
Everything his father had given him,
Not one single thing he left.
He then went on his journey,
Just following after his star
Trying to make a living
In another land so far.
He lived wildly and wastefully,
And all his money he did spend.
He became so very poor,
He fed swine there at the end.
This was a very lowly job,
Especially for a Hebrew man
But he was trying to survive
In that distant far off land.
One day he came to himself
While feeding hogs and eating husks.
He knew his father's servants ate well,
So to go back home was a must.
He arose and went to his father
Who saw him coming from far away
And who ran out and kissed him,
That is when this son did say,

Father, I'm no longer worthy
To be called your son,
So let me be a servant to you,
Being paid when my work is done.
His father gave him a robe instead
And put a ring on his hand,
Then killed a fatted calf,
But his brother didn't understand.
This made him so very angry
That he would not go in and enjoy
This party given for his brother,
He just pouted like a little boy.
He said, Father you've never done this
For me and all my friends.
The father said, Son, you've always been here,
But your brother has come home again.
It is right that we make merry
Because we're all so very glad,
That he is alive who once was dead
And you should not be mad.
This father was compassionate
And filled with agape love,
He really was a type of Christ
Like our Lord, our Father above.

Ephesians 4:32
And be ye kind one to another, tenderhearted,
forgiving one another, even as God for Christ's sake
hath forgiven you.

The Good Samaritan

A man went down from Jerusalem
All the way to Jericho,
Not knowing that his journey
Would be filled with grief and woe.
He fell among some thieves
Who stripped him of his clothes,
Then left him there almost dead,
Bleeding from his head to his toes.
Soon there came a certain Priest
Who had just too much pride
And wouldn't stop and help this man
But passed by on the other side.
Along then came another man,
One who was a Levite,
He also kept on walking
When he came upon this sight.
It seemed no one would help him,
This man in such dire need
Until there came a Samaritan
Who did a really good deed.
He bound up all his wounds
And poured in some oil and wine,
Then set him on his own beast,
This man so good and kind.
He then took him to a place
And took good care of him
And helped this man get well
Whose outlook was once so dim.
When the Samaritan departed,
He gave money to the man of the Inn
And said, If it costs any more,
I'll pay you when I come again.

Now which of these three men
Was a good neighbor to that man
Who fell among the thieves,
Do you now understand?
It was he who showed him mercy,
Who was a neighbor in God's eyes.
This story tells each of us,
We must go out and do likewise.

<hr/>

A New World

John saw a new heaven and earth
For the old had passed away.
The Holy city of Jerusalem came down
Out of Heaven on that day.
John heard a voice saying,
God's tabernacle is with men.
These people shall be His people,
He'll be their God as He's always been.
He'll wipe the tears from their eyes,
There'll be no death, no sorrow.
Former things are all passed away
There'll be no worry about tomorrow.
Then He that sat on the throne,
Said He'd make all things new
And told John to write these words,
Which all now are tried and true.
Write I am the Alpha and the Omega,
This will help you to comprehend,
I give living waters to the thirsty,
I AM the BEGINNING and the END!

A maid was possessed with a spirit
Who would divine and soothsay,
Making much money for her masters,
And followed Paul and Silas one day.
After many days Paul was grieved
And ordered the spirit to come out,
Which it did that very same hour,
But her masters let out a shout,
Saying, These Jews are causing trouble,
Teaching customs we don't observe,
So the people rose up against them,
And the God whom they did serve.
They tore off these men's clothes
And both of them they beat,
Then cast them into prison
And shackled their hands and feet.
At midnight these two prayed
And sang praises to God their King.
Suddenly a great big earthquake
Shook the walls and everything.
The jailor found the prison door open
And pulled out his long, sharp blade,
For he was told to safeguard these men,
But thought they were gone and was afraid.
As he was about to kill himself,
Paul cried out in a loud voice.
Do not harm yourself we're here,
We did not escape, but stayed by choice.

The jailor fell down before them
And said, What must I do to be saved?
They said, Believe in Jesus Christ,
Who on the cross His life gave.
The jailor's family became Christians,
Because they believed Jesus was Lord,
And they worshipped Him and God.
The jailor was saved from death by his sword.

House on the Rock

Those who hear Jesus' words
And in them do take stock
Will be like that wise man
Who built his house upon a rock.
Then the rain descended,
Followed by a great big flood,
And the wind blew very hard
But that man's house still stood.
Those that hear His sayings
And yet do not understand
Will be like that foolish one
Who built his house upon the sand.
Again the rains came down
And someone opened the flood gate.
Strong winds blew against the house
And the fall of it was great.
We must be like the wise man
Who was very, very smart.
Then no matter what befalls us,
We'll be close to God's own heart!

Almost Persuaded

Paul was brought before Agrippa
To speak in his own defense
For things he was accused of,
But didn't do, so it made no sense.
He said, I'll answer on my behalf
Of those things of which I'm accused,
For I have been mocked and ridiculed,
And also beaten and abused.
I know you are an expert, O king,
Of all the customs of the Jews
And that you will treat me fairly
As you listen to my views.
My manner of life from a youth
Was that of a Pharisee,
And I persecuted Christians
Until they were afraid of me.
On the road to Damascus,
I met Christ, the Son of God
And there became a Christian
Just like those on whom I've trod.
I stand now being judged
For the hope of a promise made
By God to our fathers long ago,
Yes, even hundreds of decades.
In a vision my God gave me,
He told me what I must do,
And that is to preach about Jesus,
Just like I'm doing to you.
That Jesus would suffer many trials
And be crucified and buried in a cave,
But that He would come to life again
And would rise out of His grave.

I speak these words of truth to you,
Yes, I do now profess,
That Jesus is the Son of God,
And this you should confess,
For I believe that you do know
And believe what the prophets taught,
That our Messiah would come someday,
Please don't let that go for naught.
Then King Agrippa said to Paul,
Thou hast persuaded me almost,
To be a Christian just like you
And to worship your Lord of Host.

Acts 26:29

And Paul said, I would to God that not only thou, but also all that hear me this day, were both almost and altogether such as I am, except these bonds.

The Widow's Mite

Jesus sat over by the treasury
And saw how people their money cast.
Many rich people put in much
For their possessions were so vast.
Then came in a poor widow
Who cast in two mites, a farthing.
Now to those with lots of money,
This seemed like almost nothing.
But Jesus told His disciples,
This widow had put in much more
Than all the others put together
Because this woman was so poor.
They put in of an abundance,
While she gave all that she had
And even though she was in want,
She did it with a heart so glad.

Faith is the substance of things hoped for,
The evidence of things not seen.
Faith is how we understand God's Word
And know just what it means.
By faith Abel offered a sacrifice
Better than his brother Cain.
It proved he was more righteous.
That is how it was explained.
By faith Enoch was taken up
On that we all agree,
His body was never found,
God translated him, you see.
Without faith we can't please God
For we must first believe He is
And that He rewards those that seek Him,
Without question, with no quiz.
By faith Noah, being warned of God
Of things not seen as yet
Moved fearfully and built an ark
And the rest of the world got wet.
By faith Abraham, went to a place,
Not knowing where he was sent
And journeyed in that promised land.
He obeyed God, and just went.
Through faith Sarah, herself,
Received the strength to conceive
And had a child when she was old,
For God's promise she believed.

By faith Abraham offered Isaac,
His only son, without any dread,
Believing God could raise him again,
If need be from the dead.
By faith Isaac blessed his sons
Concerning things yet to come,
And Jacob when he was dying,
Blessed both of Joseph's sons.
Joseph by faith as he died
Mentioned the children of Israel,
And gave instructions about his bones
And the place where they should dwell.
By faith Moses, when he was grown
Refused to be the son of Pharaoh's daughter,
And suffered affliction by his people,
Then saved them by parting the water.
By faith the walls of Jericho
All came tumbling down
But the harlot Rahab did not perish
With the unbelievers in her town.
And what more shall be said,
There is not enough time to tell,
Of Gideon, Barak and Samson,
Of Daniel, David and Samuel,
Who by faith subdued kingdoms
And saw many promises attained
And saw the mouths of lions shut,
Which God did for His gain.
Some received their dead to life again.
Others were tortured for their belief,
Being mocked, beaten and imprisoned
And being stoned with no relief.

Many wandered in the deserts
And in the mountains high,
And in dens and caves on earth
Where so many of them did die.
All of these obtained a good report
Because of their faith we do suspect,
And God will do the same for us,
Even more than we should expect!

The Rich Young Ruler

There was a rich, young ruler
That came to Christ one day
Wanting to have eternal life,
And said, Tell me how I pray.
Jesus told him to know the laws
And not commit adultery or kill,
To honor his mother and father
And not lie, cheat or steal.
The ruler said to Him, Master,
I have done so from my youth,
And Jesus thereby loved him,
For he was telling Him the truth.
But this ruler went away grieved,
When told to give up all he had,
And take up the cross and follow Christ.
This made him so very sad,
For he had many possessions on earth
And they continued to grow.
He found out where his treasure was,
His heart was there also.

The Woman at the Well

Jesus came to a city of Samaria
And being tired sat by a well.
When a woman came and drew water,
He asked for some, His thirst to quell.
She had been there just a short time
But realized that He was a Jew.
Now they didn't deal with Samaritans,
That's something all her life she knew.
She said, How is it that a Jew
Can ask a drink from a Samaritan?
She didn't know who He was
And so she could not understand.
He said, If you knew the gift of God
And who asked a drink of thee,
He would give you living water.
You would not thirst again, you see.
Then He told her of her husbands
And many other things as well,
And she believed in Him that day
And told others where she dwelled.
Many Samaritans believed in Him
Because of the words she testified
And many more later believed
But on Christ's own words relied.
Now this woman had a great impact
Because her beliefs she did share
And she won many souls to Jesus.
So can we, if we just dare.

Water From the Rock

The children of Israel journeyed,
Out into the desert of Zin,
Where there was no water,
For Moses, his people, his kin.
The people then gathered together,
Saying, Why did you bring us here?
They were so very thirsty
And they were filled with fear.
They had followed Moses out of Egypt
And to this desert dry,
With nothing here to drink,
Not even water from the sky.
There were no pomegranates,
Nor were there any vines,
And no water anywhere,
There also was no wine.
Moses was told by God
To assemble everyone
And speak to the rock before him,
Water would come out once that was done.
Moses didn't do as he was told,
But struck the stone with his rod
And because of his unbelief
He really angered God.
Yet the water did flow freely
For Moses and all his band
But his brazen disobedience,
Kept them out of the Promised Land.
So when God gives us an order
To do something a certain way,
We had better do it just like He says,
Or there'll be consequences to pay.

Zacchaeus

As Jesus passed through Jericho
Zacchaeus, a Publican,
Really wanted to see Him
But he was shorter than any man.
Although he was short in stature
He was very big in heart
And gave many goods to the poor,
Doing much more than his part.
So he ran up far ahead
And climbed a Sycamore tree,
He needed to get high enough,
This Son of God to see.
Jesus looked up and saw him
And said, Zacchaeus come down in haste,
For I'm going to dine with you.
There was no time to waste.
So he came down right away
And although he was a sinner,
Since Jesus was going to his house,
He must have felt like a winner.
When the other people heard this,
They stood there and complained
That if Jesus ate with this sinner
His reputation would be stained.
Jesus told Zacchaeus, Salvation,
Was this day come to his home
And that he would never lose it,
Even when Christ's Kingdom was come.

Now Saul was fully consenting
To having Stephen stoned
And even stood there watching
As the rocks broke all his bones.
He continued to make havoc
Of the Church and Christian men
By putting them in prison and,
Persecuting them over and over again.
One day on the road to Damascus
A light from Heaven shined about.
Saul fell down to the earth,
Hearing a voice, almost a shout.
It was the voice of the God saying,
Saul, Why do you persecute me?
As Saul got up off the ground
He was as blind as he could be.
Saul was filled with great fear
And said, Lord what must I do?
He was told to go to the city,
But just why he had no clue.
They took him to Damascus,
Leading him by his hand
And he was blind for three full days;
This he could not understand.
The Lord then told Ananias
To go out and find Saul
And make him see again,
And Ananias heeded God's call.

Saul would preach to the Gentiles
And to Israel and the kings.
He would suffer for God's sake
And do many wonderful things.

Ananias went to the house
Just so that he might,
Lay his hands on Saul
And help him receive his sight.

Saul was filled with the spirit,
Then what happened was hard to tell,
For something fell from his eyes
And now he could see so well.

He was taken to a near place
Where he was baptized,
And as he came out of the water,
It was a new man that did arise.

There was an amazing change,
In this man named Saul,
For he was now a Christian
And God changed his name to Paul.

Right away he preached about Jesus
As being the only Son of God
And he no longer killed the Jews
With his sword and rod.

Paul won souls to Jesus Christ
And also opened many a door,
For those who came after him,
To win many, many more.

Romans 6:6

> *Knowing this, that our old man is crucified with Him, that the body
> of sin might be destroyed, that henceforth we should not serve sin.*

Shadrack, Meshack and Abednego

In the days of King Nebuchadnezzar
There were three God fearing men
Who obeyed their God completely,
And promised Him they would not sin.
They were very loyal to their king
And always willing and able
To serve him in any way,
But would not eat from his table.
They would not defile their bodies
With red meat, or the drinking of wine
And these three stayed strong and healthy
And everything was going just fine,
Until one day when their king
Filled with pride and without any shame,
Made images and idols of gold,
And ordered his people to worship the same.
He said those who failed to do so
Would be cast in the furnace of fire,
Thinking this would please his ego
And fulfill his selfish desire.
At the hour when the music sounded
All the people had to bow down
And worship the graven images
Of the king who wore the crown.
But Shadrack, Meshack and Abednego
Did not do as they were told,
So the king was very angry at them
For being so brash and bold.

He was filled with hatred and rage
And about to unleash his fury
On these who had disobeyed him,
He would be their judge and jury.
He said, When the music is sounded,
In that instant that very same hour,
You'll be chained and thrown in the furnace,
And I'll stand by and watch you cower.
Do you think your God will be able
To keep you alive in that place?
Yes, O king, they replied,
Because of His power, mercy and grace,
But if He chooses to let us perish
We want the entire world to know
That He still is the only true God
And we know He loves us so.
The music finally sounded
And the three again refused
To bow down to the king's images
So now they must pay their dues.
The king commanded his servants
To heat the furnace seven times more.
The heat was so great it killed the men
Who tossed them through the furnace door.
Shadrack, Meshack and Abednego
Were in the mist of flames so hot
And the king was very anxious
To see if they were being consumed, or not.
He looked in and was very astounded
And called his counselors to come see,
There was a fourth man in the furnace,
But they had tossed in only three.

None of these men were chained
But each one shackle free,
Walking around on those red hot coals,
Impossible! How could that be?
But the king believed what he saw
And the others agreed with head nods
That there was a fourth man in there
With a form like the son of the gods.
The king called out to them saying,
Come out of there and come here
And the three came out as ordered
And stood before him without any fear.
Their clothes showed no signs of scorching
And not a hair on their head was singed.
This was so very unbelievable
The king almost became "unhinged"
He said, Blessed be the God of Shadrack,
Meshack and Abednego,
Who protected them in that furnace
For being faithful and trusting Him so.
He then gave a decree to his people
Of every city, country and port,
Not to speak evil of their God
Who did great miracles of this sort.
So Shadrack, Meshack and Abednego
Found favor with the king that day,
Because they trusted God completely
And knew He would have His way.
Let us learn a lesson from these three
And do exactly as they, you and I,
And in the face of adversity
On God we can always rely!

Life here on this earth
Is just a journey my friend,
A journey which someday
Will come to an end,
At a fork in the road
Where only you can decide
The place in eternity
Where you will reside.
One road is narrow
But is the right way,
The one you should follow
And on which you should stay.
The other road beckons
For it is so wide
But it leads to destruction
With every stride.
The narrow road is God's
So please choose it early
For it leads right up to
Those gates white and pearly.
The wide road surely
Should hold no desire
For it leads to eternal
Damnation and fire.
If you've gone through life
And not chosen a road.
Do it right now
For it will lighten your load.
The narrow road to Heaven
It must be the one
Because it was built by the blood
Of God's only Son.
So choose the right road
It is never too late.
Jesus is waiting
At those Heavenly gates.

The Comfort of a Mother's Love

All of my life she has blessed me
With the comfort of love so sweet.
Her presence and prayers inspire me,
She helps make my life complete.
She is always an encouragement,
Which is what a child does need.
She has provided a safe haven
And has helped me to succeed.
Her love is inexhaustible
Like that of our Lord Jesus,
Who put Himself on that cross
And gave His life for us.
But now she's getting older
And not as agile as she has been
And she has become forgetful
Because her mind is not as keen.
I know one day she'll leave me
But I know that's when her Lord
Will take her gently by her hand
And lead her to her reward.
Yes, He'll walk her to that mansion,
That Heavenly home where she will dwell.
For those of us who know Jesus,
It will be our home as well.
A Mother's love is so comforting
And it is unconditional love,
That will last for all eternity
Like that of God in Heaven above.

(This poem was inspired by an e-mail from Pastor Tim Dowdy to his church family, informing them of the sudden and untimely death of his sweet mother. It was first written as a sympathy card, and then later adapted for use in this book with his permission.)

Jericho

Joshua won the battle of Jericho
By marching around that town
Once a day for three whole days
And his men made not one sound.
The Ark of the Lord went up ahead.
Seven priests sounded on rams' horns.
They did this each and everyday
Until the day of the seventh morn.
His people circled Jericho seven times
And the people inside had no idea,
Of what was going to happen to them
But to Joshua it was very clear.
On the seventh march around Jericho
They heard trumpets blow without,
Then Joshua gave the order
For his people all to shout.
They did as they were told
And great noise did abound,
So great that it shook that city
And the walls came tumbling down.
Joshua then took that city
And it gives my heart a thrill,
To see the miracles God does today,
When His people stay in His will.

David and Bathsheba

David was a man after God's own heart,
That is what the scriptures say
But that all changed with one glance
On a clear but fateful day.
That's when David woke up early
And went out on his high roof top,
Then spied Bathsheba bathing herself.
This sight made his heart flip, flop.
As he stood there gaping at her
Everything would have been just fine
If he had turned and looked away
And gotten this picture out of his mind.
But we know he didn't do that
But sent his men down to inquire,
Which fanned the flame even more
Increasing his lustful desire.
He told his servants to go get her
And bring her straight to him,
Which displeased God very much
And His anger filled up to the brim.
God sent Nathan with a story
About two men in one city.
One was a very rich man,
And the other poor, what a pity.
The rich man had many sheep
But the poor man had just one,
That he had raised from a lamb
And was proud of what he had done.
His lamb grew up with his children
And ate and drank from his own cup,
But the rich man took that sheep
To feed a traveler who came to sup.

Nathan asked King David
Just what he would do,
To the man who had many sheep
But took the poor man's only ewe?
Now David felt much anger at this
And said that rich man he must die
For taking the poor man's only sheep
And having no good reason why.
So Nathan said to David
You have sealed your own fate
For you are that rich man
And have done what God does hate.
You have many wives
But your servant had just one,
Then you took her from him
And had him slain once that was done.
Now God really punished David
Yet refused to take his life,
But took the life of his only son,
He had by another man's wife.
David then asked God's forgiveness
For the time he misbehaved
And God blessed his servant again
And very quickly forgave.
Let us learn a lesson from David
And when we have committed a sin,
Quickly ask for God's forgiveness
And get in fellowship again.

Proverbs 27:20b

so the eyes of man are never satisfied.

Hebrews 13:5b

and be content with such things as you have:
for I will never leave you, nor forsake you.

Moses

A new Pharaoh arose over Egypt
Who said all male Jew babies must die,
For there are already too many of them
And they continue to multiply.
Moses was born soon after that
And him his mother did hide,
For three months, then built an ark
Of bulrushes and put him inside.
Pharaoh's daughter found Moses
And claimed him as her own.
The wet nurse she chose was his mother,
Who raised him until he was grown.
He became a brother to Ramses
But knew his own people were slaves
And got angry when he saw an Egyptian,
Beating them with whips and staves.
When he thought no one was looking
He slew him and hid him in the sand,
But Pharaoh soon got word of this
And Moses fled to another land.
That's where he met God face to face
At a burning bush not being consumed.
When God called out his name,
He must have felt like he was doomed.
He was told not to come near
And to take the sandals off his feet
For where he stood was Holy ground.
That's how he and God did meet.

Moses was to lead his people out of Egypt
To a land filled with milk and honey,
Out of the dark days of slavery
To a promised land free and sunny.
Now Moses didn't feel qualified
And in his own mind did perceive,
That although he was sent by God
His people would not believe.
Yet, he went as God commanded
And God did miracles you know
Such as frogs, hail and locusts,
But Pharaoh wouldn't let His people go.
One more miracle was needed
To make Pharaoh change his mind,
So God would kill all the first born
In every house, which seemed unkind.
Then it came to pass at midnight,
The firstborn though-out the land,
Except in homes with lambs' blood,
Were smote by God's own hand.
Even Pharaoh's firstborn was slain
So he sent for Moses by night,
And said, Come and get your people,
Pharaoh wanted them out of his sight.
Moses then led them out of Egypt
Through the wilderness to the sea
And God was with them all the way,
Just as close as He could be.
He was in a pillar of clouds by day
And in a pillar of fire by night,
Always going before His people
Seeing that things went right.

But Pharaoh's heart was hardened again
And his people made quite a fuss,
Saying, Why did you let them go,
They should still be serving us.
So Pharaoh took all his chariots,
For he regretted what he had done
And went out after those people,
To catch and bring back every one.
He thought that he had caught them
Down by a sea named Red
But Moses cried out to God
Who said, Send them on ahead.
God told Moses to lift up his rod,
Then to stretch out his hand.
The sea would be divided
And they could cross it on dry land.
Then Pharaoh's people would know
That He was the mighty Lord,
Because they would die more quickly
Than being struck down by the sword.
So Moses' people went through the sea
And walls of water were left and right
But they just kept on walking,
Though many were filled with fright.
As Pharaoh's army followed,
God removed their chariots wheels
And they could hardly move.
Can you imagine how that feels?
Again God spoke to Moses
Who stretched his hand toward the sea,
Then the water covered the Egyptians
And not a single one got free.

Now God saved His people Israel
And Pharaoh's entire army drowned.
The Israelites believed God once more
And to Him became honor bound.

Pillar Of Salt

Sodom was a very wicked place
That God planned to destroy
And sent some angels to warn Lot,
To leave the city, that was their ploy.
Now it was such an evil town
And was so very full of sin,
And an abomination to the Lord,
For men were seeking after men.
The angel took Lot by the hand
And too, the hand of his wife,
Then took them out of the city
In order to save each life.
They said, Go on through the plain
And to those mountains high
And whatever you do, don't look back,
If you do you'll surely die.
God then rained fire and brimstone
Upon both Sodom and Gomorrah,
And Lot's wife didn't know this
But she would never see tomorrow.
She just had to take one last look,
So it was really her own fault,
That when she disobeyed God,
She became a pillar of salt.

Jacob's Ladder

Jacob had a dream one night
Of a ladder from earth to the sky.
The top of it reached Heaven,
He just didn't understand why.
There were angels going up
And also angels coming down.
The Lord was standing up above,
Who said, I'm the God of Abraham.
The ground on which Jacob lay
Would be for him and his seed,
Also the north, east, south and west.
God would meet his every need.
All his families would be blessed
And his seed would spread as dust.
God would always be there with him
This is one thing he could trust.
Jacob knew this was God's house
And made an altar of stone right there
And God showered him with blessings,
Showing Jacob His love and care.
Jacob named that place Bethel,
Which one time was called Luz,
And promised God a tenth of all he had,
That's just the way it "wuz".

The people of Israel were unhappy
And they did not pass God's test,
Of being in this forsaken land,
And they got into a mess.
First, they murmured against Moses
And then spoke against their Lord.
Who sent many firey serpents,
As their fair and just reward.
These serpents bit many people
Causing some of them to die,
And no one could avoid them
No matter how hard they'd try
So the people came to Moses,
And said, against our Lord we've sinned.
Please ask Him to destroy these snakes
And give us His blessings again.
God told Moses to make a brass serpent
And put it on top of a pole,
And when a snake bitten man looked on it,
He would not die, but be made whole.
So when we, like them, see our sin
And go to God and confess.
He'll forgive us as He forgave them,
And our lives will be greatly blessed.

1 John 1:9

If we confess our sins, He is faithful and just to forgive
us our sins, and to cleanse us from all unrighteousness.

At the time when Herod was king
He afflicted the Church of the Lord.
He killed James the brother of John
And did it with his own sword.

When he saw this pleased the Jews,
He had Peter thrown in Jail
And would kill him on the morrow,
If everything went along well.

While Peter was in that prison,
Prayers for him did not cease.
The Church and all it's people
Were asking God for his release.

On the night before he was to die,
Peter was lying there sleeping,
Bound with chains between two guards,
While two others the doors were keeping.

Then an angel of the Lord came
And there shined a bright light
The angel then smote Peter.
It was now time to take flight.

The angel said, Arise quickly,
And the chains fell off his hands.
He told Peter to put on his sandals,
It was time for him to stand.

He was told to put on his clothes
And Peter did as he was told,
Not knowing at this time,
An angel made this scene unfold.

He thought he was in a vision
Or maybe having a dream.
What was happening was very real
And he was surprised it seems.
They passed the first and second guards
And then came to an iron gate,
That opened of its own accord,
This was done by God, not fate!
Here we see God doing the impossible,
That which couldn't be done by man,
Like loosening Peter's shackles
From his feet and hands.
But He then let Saint Peter
Do those things which he could do,
Such as putting on his clothes
And putting on each shoe.
Do you think maybe this tells us,
God wants us to do what we can do,
Then He will do all those things
That are impossible for me and you?

Acts 12:7b

And his chains fell off his hands.

Acts 12:8

*And the angel said unto him, gird thyself,
and bind on thy sandals, and so he did.*

The Tower of Babel

The people all spoke one language,
Just one tongue after the flood.
They could understand each other,
Which would soon end with a thud.
The people journeyed eastward
To a plain and dwelt there.
They were all very happy.
And did not seem to have a care
They took some brick and mortar,
And began to build a city
With a tower to reach the heavens,
Something they soon would pity.
They did not want to be scattered,
So they would make themselves a name.
God was not pleased with this,
Yet, they did it just the same.
The Lord came down to see
This city with its tall tower
And realized men on earth
Had far too much power.
He said, They are all one people
And only one language they use.
Now nothing is impossible for them,
We must make them all confused.
The Lord scrambled their speech
And no more could they understand
What men around them were saying
And scattered them across the land.

There was much confusion now
And things would never be the same.
They gave up on building the city
And the tower of Babel, as it was named.
Since men were beginning to think,
That they were such a powerful race
And had no need for God anymore,
He just put them in their place.

Proverbs 28:26

He that trusteth in his own heart is a fool:
but whoso walketh wisely, he shall be delivered.

Mustard Seed

The Kingdom of Heaven is like
A tiny grain of mustard seed,
Which a man takes and sows,
It is the smallest seed indeed.
When it becomes fully grown
It is so very, very big,
It is the greatest of all herbs
And birds land in its twigs.
Now if we can have the faith
Of that tiny grain of seed,
God will take care of us
And meet our every need.

When Naomi's husband died,
He left her with two sons.
What she did not know was
Her troubles had just begun.
The sons took themselves wives.
One named Orpah, one named Ruth.
Both of the sons later died.
That is the awful truth.
There was a famine in the land
And there was no food to eat,
So these women went to Moab,
Traveling there on their feet.
Naomi told each daughter-in-law
To return to the home of her mother,
Where she would be better off,
Than in the house of any other.
So Orpah kissed Naomi goodbye
And then quickly turned and went,
But Ruth would not leave her,
And her decision was so intent.
She said, Where you go I will go
And where you lodge, I will too
I will never ever leave
Because I want to be with you
Your people will be my people
And I will serve the God you love.
He will deal very kindly with you
And share His blessings from above.

Where you die, I will die
For I love you with all my heart.
Nothing can ever separate us,
Only death can bring us apart.
Ruth would not leave Naomi
And took care of her friend so kind
And was with her to the very end.
Such loyalty is hard to find.

False Teachers

Be careful what you listen to
Then mull over what you hear,
For many preachers of this day
Seem to have no Godly fear.
They always use the Bible
As they claim to preach God's Word
But it's often not the Gospel truth
Just false doctrines that you've heard.
Scriptures tell us that in latter days
Men will leave their faith behind
And speak lies in hypocrisy,
Because of the searing of their mind.
So don't be fooled by false teachings
But establish your heart in grace.
Keep your eyes stayed on Christ
And you'll be in a righteous place.

2 Timothy 4:4

*And they shall turn their ears from the
truth, and shall be turned to fables.*

There was a man that had two wives
And one had daughters and sons.
God had closed the other's womb
So she had not a single one.
Her husband treated her kindly;
Hannah was this wife's name,
And even though she was barren,
He loved her just the same.
But the other wife provoked her
Until she made poor Hannah weep.
Her husband tried to console her
For he knew her pain was deep.
Am I not better than ten sons?
He asked her in her grief
But she had so much bitterness
His words were of no relief.
At the temple Hannah prayed
And to God she made a vow
If you will give me the son I want,
I'll give him back to you even now.
Eli the priest saw her lips move
But did not hear one sound,
And figured she was drunk with wine,
And this caused the priest to frown.
The Holy one said to her,
How long have you been drunk?
When Hannah heard these words
Her heavy heart just sunk.

She said, I'm a woman of sorrow
And have not been drinking wine,
If I could have a baby boy
My spirits would be just fine.
May God grant this petition
That you have asked of Him.
Now Eli's words were comforting,
But her chances seemed so slim.
Yet, God was busy working
And opened up her womb,
And she had the baby, Samuel;
He was like a flower in bloom.
She kept him away from the temple
Until the day that he was weaned,
Then went and gave her son to God
And so kept her vow it seemed.
Eli was there and she told him,
The Lord God heard my plea,
Now I am giving back to Him,
The young son that He gave me.
Samuel ministered in the temple
From his youth to his old age,
But to tell all that this man did
Would take more than another page.
Samuel served God daily,
And wore a robe; a shroud.
He not only brought his mother joy
But made his Lord very proud.

Don't Mourn for Me

Don't mourn for me for all is well,
I am not here, it is only my shell.
I am now in Heaven with Jesus Christ
Who died for me and paid the price,
So Heaven's gates I could enter in
Even though my life had much sin.
I am now walking those streets of gold,
Seeing great wonders before me unfold.
As you read this poem I hope and I pray,
That you know Jesus is the only way
To get up to Heaven when you die,
There's no other way, it's just Satan's big lie.

A Special Promise Verse

Romans 10:9.

*That if thou wilt confess with thy mouth
the Lord Jesus, and believe in thine heart that God
has raised him from the dead, thou shalt be saved.*

(This is a special verse because it is the promise from God I chose the day I got saved. My "born again" birth certificate, and proof that I am His.)

Love at Calvary, Jesus died for me,
Washed away my sin, new life did begin.
Love at Calvary, Jesus on that tree,
Hung upon that cross; just to save the lost.
Jesus was the only way, God could reconcile,
Change me from my sinful ways,
And make me His child.
Love at Calvary, purposed just for me,
You can have the same, just call on His name,
Just call on His name.

The Lord is Nigh

The Lord is nigh unto all
Who in truth to Him call,
He'll fulfill the desires of their heart.
To all them who fear
He'll wipe away every tear.
He loved them right from the start.
Yes, God loves everyone
Who lives under His sun
And He is always very nigh.
Though times may seem tough
And life really gets rough,
He'll care for your needs by and by.

James 4:8

Draw nigh unto God and He will draw nigh to thee.

When Tragedy Strikes

The way to respond when tragedy strikes
Is to show love that is Christ-like,
And forget ourselves and in selflessness,
Turn to those that are in distress.
We must have courage, and determination,
And cry out to God for His confirmation.
Then be calm though the heartache and pain
And trust in Him so our prayers aren't in vain.
We must ask God in silence or out loud,
The reason why this thing was allowed.
And as we seek comfort from the Lord,
Focus on Him and His Holy Word.
Pray that our leaders respond Godly and bold
And that justice comes quickly for He's in control.
This tragedy is evil but God meant it for good.
Our burdens will lighten once that's understood.
That is our promise in Romans eight twenty eight,
If we'll just believe that, it will lift a great weight.
All things happen for good to them that love the Lord.
That's God promise to us in His Holy Word!

(This poem and the two following were adapted from notes of sermons preached by Dr. Charles Stanley shortly after the September 11, 2001 attacks, and are used with permission.)

There was a cloud of uncertainty
Hanging over our great land,
Caused by the evil actions
Of an infidel of a man.
Our response to September eleventh,
Was much shock and disbelief,
And fear, anger and confusion
With deep, abiding grief.
Those who lost loved ones,
Felt empty and incomplete
But will overcome those feelings,
And so accomplish quite a feat.
God will never forsake them
But will be with them to the end.
He'll give them strength to draw on
For He is a true and caring friend.
Now a part of them is missing
And there's a sense of deep regret
Of things they said or didn't say
And there are needs that are not met.
The hurt has settled deep inside
And not easy to talk about,
Yet, must not be kept within
But opened up and let out.
We must accept the fact it happened
Causing much sorrow and much pain,
And avoid denial and anger
And depression and energy drain.
Our comfort in this affliction
Is the truth in God's Word, you see,
Which is unyielding love and peace,
That He gives to you and me.

When we accept our circumstances
God will comfort us in a way,
That we can comfort others
As we live from day to day,
By loving them, and listening,
And keeping confident what they share.
By helping to meet their needs
And showing them that we care.
We must put all our trust in God
And remember He loves us so.
He will always be there with us
No matter where we go!

Unshakable Faith

To have unshakable faith
In these uncertain times
Means we must not waver
But we must by design,
Keep our focus on God
And see things through His eyes,
And be anchored in His truth
And not in Satan's lies.
We must have a strong conviction
That our Lord God rules,
And has a plan for each of us
And even has the tools,
To take care of the hardships
That befall both you and me,
And know He's in control
Like no one else can be.

When we honestly face
Our suffering and our pain
And keep our focus on God,
Our faith will surely remain.
Our faith it must not falter
As we continue to strive
And His powerful love
Will help us all survive.
When we face our enemy
We must not show fear,
Though much evil beset us
Our God is always near.
Any fear will be fleeting
It just will not hang around,
If we'll only trust in God,
His peace will abound.
These uncertain times
Will most surely abate
As we feed on His Word
And as we meditate.
We know unshakable faith
Will always find a way,
When there seems to be none
If we simply just obey.
We must trust God completely
In those times of despair,
Then in the face of adversity
God will always be there.

God sent the angel Gabriel
To tell Mary she'd have God's child
But since she was a virgin,
This must have made her smile.
She would call His name Jesus,
For He would take away man's sin.
He would reign over His Kingdom,
To which there would be no end.
Joseph saw Mary was with child
And was going to put her away,
But God told him to marry her
And his Lord he did obey.
He'd be the Saviour of the world
From the day that He was born.
That day would be celebrated
With gifts, and trees adorned.
He would also be a carpenter,
Making things with His hands,
Until they were nailed to the cross,
And now men must take a stand.
They must believe He did it for them,
With Heaven being their desire,
Or not believe and end up in
Satan's pit of blazing fire.

The Tower of "Babble"

There is a modern day tower
That picks up signals in the sky
And can spread the Gospel message
In the twinkling of an eye.
The Good News can be sent
To every city and its people,
From these towers everywhere
That look much like a steeple.
But be warned they also
Carry much filth and sin
And if we're not real careful
We'll be deceived and sucked in.
They send signals to our cell phones,
Which at times are not so clear
And when we try to call someone
We have to ask them, Can you hear?
Sometimes to get a good signal
We struggle and we scrabble
And talk our sometimes-foolish talk.
Could this be the Tower of "Babble»?

Can you hear me now?
        CAN YOU HEAR ME NOW?
                CAN YOU HEAR ME NOW?

Sarah Laughed

When God promised Sarah a son,
She laughed within when she was told,
Thinking this would never happen
Because she was now so very old.
The angels outside heard her
And she was rebuked by the Lord,
But Abraham loved God so much,
A son would be his just reward.
This happened sometime later
And Sarah had that promised child.
Abraham was one hundred years old
And to us that might seem wild,
But it just proves to God's people
There is not anything He can't do
And whatever He plans in life for us
He has the power to see it through.

Luke 9:43a

And they were all amazed at the power of God.

2 Samuel 22:33

God is my strength and my power: and makes my way perfect.

Because of Paul's appeal to Caesar
He had to be sent to Rome
Where he would stand trial,
So far away from home.
It would be a very long journey,
Which would be made by ship
And several other prisoners
Would also make that trip.
They sailed by the coast of Asia
Stopping at a place named Sidon.
The centurion trusted Paul enough
To let him visit some friends alone.
Shortly after the ship left there
The winds became contrary,
But the ship had to get to Rome
So kept its course and did not vary.
The waves were high and rough
And caused the ship to wrestle,
Against them just to stay afloat,
So they decided to change vessels.
They sailed again for many days
And went by a place called Crete.
The ship was tossed about so much
That the men on board were "beat".
Sailing was too dangerous now
So the captain, Paul did alert,
Saying, The ship will be damaged
And the men will all be hurt.

The centurion didn't believe him
And wanted to seek a safer haven,
But the pounding waves continued
And the ship was misbehaving.
It was still driven by strong winds,
Even though they lowered the sails,
So they had to lighten the load
And maybe had some water to bail.
Now Paul had kept his silence,
But now said, had you listened to me,
We'd safe in the harbor
And not in this turbulent sea.
He said there would be no life lost
And they should be of good cheer.
This is what an angel had told him,
To help eliminate their fear.
But those on board were still afraid
And getting ready to jump ship,
But Paul told them to stay on board,
And not to give him any "lip".
They did as they were told
And sat down to bread and meat,
Then lightened the ship some more
By tossing out all the wheat.
They again sailed out to sea,
This time running the ship aground
And the aft part was broken up,
But the fore part stayed real sound.
They were going to kill the prisoners
To make sure they didn't escape
But the centurion wouldn't let them,
He had to keep Paul in good shape.

The centurion told all on board,
Jump off and swim if you can,
Otherwise grab a piece of wood
So you can make it to dry land.
Each man got there in one piece
Exactly like Paul had said,
But if they hadn't heeded his words,
They'd be at the bottom of the sea instead.

Doubting Thomas

All the disciples but Thomas, saw Jesus.
He wasn't there when Jesus came,
So he doubted they had seen Him
Or that He even called their name.
Thomas saw Jesus on the cross,
Then buried, where He should be yet,
So it was hard for him to believe
And right now his mind was set.
He said, Until I see Him myself
And touch the nail prints, and His side,
I won't believe you saw Him
And the disciples he did chide.
Then Jesus came before Thomas,
Who touched Christ's hands with his finger,
Then thrust his hand into His side
And his doubt no longer lingered.
Thomas had now seen Jesus
And knew he hadn't been deceived.
Bless-ed are those who have not seen,
Yet, have trusted and believed.

Paul survived a shipwreck
And was on an island called Melita,
Where a barbarous people lived
But not pigmies that would "eat ya".
They showed him much kindness
And even built him a fire,
Because with his wet clothes,
His need for heat was very dire.
As Paul laid sticks on the flames
A poisonous viper bit his hand,
So the tribe thought he was a murderer
And were frightened of this man.
Paul shook the snake into the fire
And since he was not harmed,
They now thought he was a god
And were no longer alarmed.
He left this quaint island
And much later arrived in Rome,
Where he dwelt for two years
In his own nice rented home.
Every day he preached about Jesus,
From early morning till the eve
And all the people heard him
But most did not believe.
The hearts of the Jews were cold,
Yet he preached for a long, long while,
But finally he just cut them off
And took God's message to the Gentiles.

Joseph

When Joseph was a young lad,
Just seventeen years old,
He had ten older brothers
Who treated him very cold.
They knew their father loved him more
For being the son of his old age,
Which triggered a lot of hate in them
That filled their hearts with rage.
And when Jacob made Joseph a coat
Of many colors, oh so bright,
Their jealousy increased so much
They couldn't stand him in their sight.
Just when they were convinced
Things couldn't get any worse,
Joseph had two dreams one night
That to them was like a curse.
He told them they would worship him,
And he said it with much pride,
And that even his father would bow down,
Now they wanted to "tan his hide"!
Then Jacob sent Joseph once more
To his brothers tending the flock
And Joseph didn't know it
But he was in for quite a shock.
His brothers planned to kill him
But threw him in a dry well instead
And were going to leave him there,
Knowing he would soon be dead.

But they sold him to some Ishmeelites
Who took him down to Egypt.
They only got twenty coins for him
So, wow, did they get gypped!
They then deceived their father
By taking him Joseph's colorful coat,
After tearing it and ripping it
And dipping it in the blood of a goat.
Jacob mourned so much for his son,
Whom he assumed was dead,
That his grief wreaked havoc on him,
Sending him to his bed.
But Joseph was down in Egypt
Working for the captain of the guard,
Who thought the world of him
For being honest and working so hard.
Now Potiphar's wife fell in love
And had a crush on this young man,
But he ran out of her presence,
Leaving his garment in her hand.
She then lied to her husband
Who sent Joseph straight to jail,
But the Lord was there with him
And the jailor treated him well.
Then Pharaoh's butler and baker
Each had a dream one night
And Joseph interpreted them both
And it turned out he was right.
The butler was restored to his old job
But the baker was hanged from a tree.
Pharaoh himself had a dream
And it remained a mystery,

Till the butler told Pharaoh about Joseph
And someone to fetch him was sent
And Joseph quickly told the king
Exactly what his dream meant.
Pharaoh was pleased, and made Joseph
Ruler over Egypt, and all the land,
And took a ring off his finger
And put it on Joseph's hand.
The seven good years prophesied went by
With plenty of crops being put in store,
Followed by seven years of famine
But they had plenty of food as before.
Joseph opened all the storehouses
For other people who needed corn,
And his brothers, all but Benjamin,
Came from the land where he was born.
They then bowed down before him
Just as they had in his dreams
And he knew them right away,
But they didn't know him it seems.
He didn't tell them who he was
And to make a long story short,
He gave them a very hard time
By pulling tricks of every sort.
He hid money in their donkey bags
And once his silver chalice.
He then accused them of theft,
With much forethought and malice.
Joseph later felt sorry for this
And decided to make himself known.
He said, I was a child when you sold me
But now I'm a man full grown.

He showed them kindness and mercy
And sat down with them to dine.
He got news about all his family
So he now felt really fine.
He loved his brothers dearly
And showed them his deep love
By forgiving each one of them,
Just like his God in Heaven above.
When Pharaoh heard about this
He was as happy as he could be
And sent horses, wagons and chariots,
To go get Joseph's family.
So his family was reunited.
His mother, father and kin,
And lived happily together in Egypt
Rejoicing over and over again.
It turned out that what happened to Joseph,
Was truly a very good thing,
For everyone was now so happy,
His family and even the king.
Joseph now told his brothers
In a way they understood,
What they once meant for evil,
God always meant for good.
This story to me has good morals,
Not just a single, but a double:
One is that being too prideful
Will get you in a lot of trouble.
But two, if you remain steadfast in God
In everything you do,
He will not only bless you,
But many others too!

According to the scriptures
Christ died for every sin
And He was dead and buried
But He rose up again.
He was first seen by Cephas,
Then also by the twelve,
And by five hundred at one time,
Then by James and Paul themselves.
Paul said he was the least of the disciples
And not worthy to be called one
For he persecuted Christians
From dawn till setting sun.
Yet God bestowed His grace on him
Which surely was not a loss
For he preached Christ more than they,
And how He died upon that cross.
He told how Christ was buried
But then came out of the grave.
Yes, how He came to life again
So every person could be saved.
How is it you disciples now say
There was no resurrection?
You need to look at God's Word
And do a little dissection.
If, in fact, Christ did not rise,
Our preaching was all for naught
And there will be no eternal life
And only lies you have taught.

You are now false witnesses
Because you have testified
That God raised Jesus from the dead
Three days after He had died.
You now say the dead cannot rise,
If so, Christ cannot be raised,
And you are still in your sins
And God cannot be praised.
Those who are asleep in Christ
Are just dead and there's no hope,
That they will ever rise again,
With that we'd have to cope.
But, Christ is raised from the dead,
He's the first fruit of them that slept.
It is truly God's great gift to us
And a truth that can't be kept.
As in Adam all men die
And this life comes to an end,
But in Christ we are made alive
For He has taken away our sin.
Behold, I show you a mystery,
All won't die but will be changed,
In the twinkling of an eye,
That's what God has pre-arranged.
The dead shall be raised incorruptible,
Others will meet Christ in the air
And they will have eternal life
In Heaven and see God there.
So our great promise is victory,
Over death, which will have no sting.
Therefore, we must give thanks to God
And to Jesus Christ our King!

Three wise men from the east
Followed a star toward Bethlehem
To see the Christ born King of the Jews,
For they wanted to worship Him.
King Herod heard about these men
And was troubled by all this.
He called his counselors to him
And to them he did insist,
That they find out where this child was,
The place where He was born,
For He would be a ruler one day
And the king was so forlorn.
His counselors said, In Bethlehem,
Is what the prophets wrote,
And this is what they said,
But it's not a perfect quote.
O, thou city of Bethlehem,
Thou surely are not the least
Of all the cities in Judah
And you'll have the Prince of Peace.
The prophets said He'd be Governor
And over all Israel He would rule.
Herod called the wise men to him
And these men he tried to fool.
He said, Go and find this child
And send word back to me,
That I may go and see Him
And worship Him myself, you see.

The wise men then departed
Following that same star
And it led them to the stable
In that distant land so far.
When they went into that place
They fell and worshipped the child,
And gave gifts of frankincense and myrrh
And maybe laid their gold in a pile.
God gave these three a warning
Not to go back to King Herod,
For he wanted to kill Jesus,
This child, the Son of God.
When they left for their country
They went back another way
And Jesus stayed alive until,
He hung on the cross that day.

Christmas Tree Lights

Christmas trees light the night
Just like that star that shone so bright
And led the wise men to the stall,
To the baby Jesus so very small.
In a manger was our Saviour born
On a day we know as Christmas morn.
Our awesome God who reigns above
Chose His only Son to show His love,
For you and me and other men
So we'd have forgiveness for our sin.
Life everlasting was His purpose you see,
When He put His gift, Jesus, on that tree.
But a gift is not yours until it's in your hand.
You must reach out and take it, you understand,
And then joy and peace will come your way.
May it happen to you this very day.

The Golden Fleece

Gideon said unto the Lord,
If you'll save Israel by my hand
I need to have a sign from you,
I sure hope you understand.
I will take a fleece of wool
And lay it on the floor,
If there is dew on it tomorrow
I won't doubt you any more.
If the earth around it is dry
I'll know that you will save,
Israel, as you have promised
And I'll be bold and brave.
Gideon woke up the next day
And wrung water out of the wool,
And kept on twisting the fleece
Until he got a whole bowl full.
Gideon again said to the Lord,
Don't let your anger toward me be hot
But next time let the fleece be dry
Without a single wet spot.
Let the ground around it
Be very wet with dew,
Then I will truly believe
You'll do what you said you'd do.
God answered Gideon's prayer
And did a miracle that night.
So Gideon was ready for battle
And would win it with God's might.

An angel spoke to Gideon,
Saying, The Lord is here with thee
O mighty man of valor
Do as I say and you will see.
Gideon rose up early
And the Lord then said to him
Your army is too large
You must give it quite a trim.
If there are too many men
They will just brag and say,
They won the battle by themselves,
God didn't help in any way.
Then Gideon told his people,
Whoever was fearful and afraid
Could return to their houses
And not take part in this raid.
Twenty two thousand left
And only ten thousand stayed,
But there were still too many,
So more cuts had to be made.
He was to take his men to the water,
Down to the well of Harod
And they would be tested there.
Not by him, but by God.

Gideon took them to the well
And would choose his men this way:
A man lapping water from his hands
Was a man that needed to stay,
But a man who drank water
While bending on his knee,
Was a man to be sent home
For he was not alert you see.
Three hundred used their hands;
God would save Israel with these men,
All the others had to leave
So this battle could begin.
Gideon divided the three hundred
Into groups one hundred strong,
And gave each man a trumpet,
Not a sword, could this be wrong?
Each man had a pitcher
And inside was a burning lamp.
Gideon said, Do just like me
Once we get outside their camp.
As they blew their trumpets
A great sound pierced the night,
Then they broke their pitchers
Which caused a very bright light.
Gideon's men shouted loudly,
The Sword of the Lord and Gideon
And the Midianites trembled with fear,
Not just a few, but every one.

Their camp was full of confusion
And among themselves they fought
And many were killed and some ran away,
But each one Gideon caught.
He killed every one of those men
Who turned and ran and fled
And his small army did the job
Just like his Lord had said.
God used Gideon to win that battle,
This man so brave and bold,
But the battle was really won
Down by that water hole.
That's where Gideon trusted God
And believed on His Holy name.
We too should be like Gideon
And always do the same.

Gideon Encouraged

When you read the story of Gideon
Whom God called a man of valor,
Yet, had to encourage him three times,
It may seem his faith was shallow.
God gave him two signs with a fleece.
First it was wet and then it was dry,
But it still was not quite enough
For this really brave tough guy.
The third time God used barley bread
Which destroyed his enemy's tent,
So no matter how strong we seem to be,
We still need God's encouragement.

Jesus stood by the lake of Gennesaret
And was being pressed by the crowd.
He saw two ships standing by
Under a sky without a cloud.
Both of these ships were empty
So he went on board one of them
And had it thrust away from shore,
Yet, the people could still hear him.
He began teaching those people
Who were standing there on land,
Listening to every single word,
Uttered by this God-sent man.
When Jesus was through speaking
He told Peter to cast his net.
Peter said, Lord we've fished all night
And haven't caught anything yet.
But Peter followed His orders.
And lowered the nets into the waters deep,
And when they brought them up again
A great harvest of fish they reaped.
Then Peter fell down at Jesus' feet
And said, I'm a sinful man, O Lord.
From that day on, he followed Him
Teaching and preaching His Word.
To Peter and the others with him
Christ said, you will be fishers of men.
They then forsook all they had
And never fished for fishes again!

Isaac was forty years old
When he took Rebekah to wife
But she didn't bear him children
And it filled this man with strife.
So he just prayed to God
To put His blessings on her
And let her give him children,
Even sons, which he'd prefer.
Pretty soon, Rebekah conceived,
After she and Isaac snuggled,
But she felt strange inside
As if her babies struggled.
God told her there were two sons
Living inside her womb.
They would be two different nations
And were trying to get more room.
They would be a different people,
One would be very strong
But the older would serve the younger
And they'd be born before long.
The first one born was hairy and red,
His voice hoarse like a grunter,
They called his name Esau
And he'd grow up to be a hunter.
Right behind came brother Jacob,
Holding on to Esau's heel
But this child was very fragile
And his skin was smooth to feel.

Now Isaac loved Esau more
Because he hunted and brought him meat.
But Rebekah loved Jacob best
For he was so clean and neat.
Esau came from the field one day,
Very tired and about to faint
And asked Jacob to give him pottage,
But Jacob said, No I can't,
Unless you give me your birthright,
Then I'll give you all you need.
Esau thought he was near death
So he very quickly agreed.
But Jacob still didn't give him food
Until he made his brother swear
That he could have his birthright,
And Esau made the vow right there.
He now hated his brother,
Yes, his brother he despised
For in a moment of weakness
He had given up his valuable prize.
Now if Esau had only waited
And maintained some self control,
He would have kept his birthright
And had many more blessings unfold.
If we are tempted like Esau,
We must trust God, and not give in,
For in His time He will meet our needs
And bless us over and over again.

Matthew 26:41
> *Watch and pray, that ye enter not into temptation:*
> *the spirit indeed is willing, but the flesh is weak.*

The Stolen Blessing

Esau gave away his birthright
And now that his father was old,
His mother plotted with Jacob
And even his blessing they stole.
They did it while Esau was hunting,
Out killing his father some meat,
And the two worked out a plan
To make their scheme complete.
Jacob would kill two kid goats
Which she would cook with flavor
And Jacob would take it to his father,
It was a meat that he would savor.
She said, He will bless you my son,
When you take that meat in there
But Jacob said, My skin is smooth,
And brother Esau has much hair.
Rebekah had thought of this also
And put skins on his hands and arms,
So when he stood next to his father
He smelled like a man from a farm.
Now Isaac heard the voice of Jacob
But felt the hair on his arms and hands
And since he was almost blind
He was fooled by this young man.
Jacob had stolen his brother's birthright
And now his blessing as well.
Esau hated his brother so much,
He vowed to kill this lad so frail.
Isaac gave his blessing to Jacob
And when Esau found out he cried.
He had lost his father's one blessing
Because his brother and mother had lied.

The Lord spoke to Gideon
Because he was not quite ready
To battle the Midianite army
For his nerves were too unsteady.
God told him to take one servant
And at night go down to the host,
And to be quiet and unseen,
Just like they were ghosts.
They got there and heard a man
Talking about his strange dream,
Which was a very weird one,
About barley bread, it seems.
The bread tumbled into their camp
And landed on top of a tent,
Smashing everything inside.
Another man knew what it meant.
He said, This is nothing else,
But Gideon and his sword,
And means we've been delivered
To Gideon, and His Lord.
Gideon went back to his camp
And was as confident as he could be,
Saying, I now know for a fact
God has given the Midianites to me.
There are times in our lives today
When God tells us something to do,
And then has to encourage us
To see that we follow through.

Jesus Betrayed

Now Satan entered into Judas,
Whose surname was Iscariot.
He was one of Jesus' disciples
But faithful he was not.
He schemed with the priests
And got money from them one day.
For just a few pieces of silver,
His Lord he would betray.

This man who was a disciple,
Was now a devil with horns,
Which he became when he took
Those thirty silver coins.
Eleven disciples were with Christ
In the garden of Gethsemane
When Judas came with the soldiers
To capture Him, you see.

The disciples who loved Jesus
Were standing by so near
And after Judas kissed Jesus,
One cut off a soldier's ear.
Then Jesus scolded that disciple
And healed the man's ear right there.
As the soldiers led Christ away,
The disciples fled, like they didn't care.

Judas took the money to the priests
For he was filled with remorse,
But they wouldn't take the money back
So he hanged himself, of course!

Peter's Denial

After Christ was betrayed by Judas
The disciples all ran away
But Peter didn't go very far,
Because he decided to stay.
He would follow them at a distance
So he would not be seen,
For if the soldiers saw him
They would treat him very mean.
Jesus was taken to the Temple
And Peter went in also,
And a maid said, He was with Jesus
But he denied this by saying, No.
Another one on the porch said,
This man was also there
But he denied knowing Christ,
And he began to swear.
Some others came over to Peter
And with confidence, said to him,
Your speech does betray you
And you are surely one of them.
Peter again swore out loud
And as his mouth let out that curse,
He once again denied Jesus,
Which made matters even worse,
For then he heard the cock crow
And knew he had denied,
Christ three times as he was told,
And he went out and bitterly cried.

God is our Keeper

Lift up your eyes unto the hills
From whence your help comes,
For it comes from the Lord,
Not just for you but for everyone.
He will not let your foot be moved,
He that keeps you will not slumber,
For He is the keeper of all men,
Not just a few in number.
He is the shade on your right hand.
The sun won't smite you by day,
Nor the moon in the night'time,
The Lord God will have His way.
He will keep you from evil
And so doing will save your soul.
He'll keep your going in and out
By the scriptures, this we're told.
We know God loves and keeps us
As we go through our daily grind,
And will always watch over us,
Just keep that in your mind.
Each one does need a keeper,
In this world so full of sin
And knowing God is with us,
Should make us smile, or grin.
Don't let the pressures of today
And your worries get you down,
For God in Heaven has set aside,
Just for you a special crown.

When Jesus was twelve years old
He went with his parents to a feast.
To the Passover at Jerusalem
And to the sacrifice of a beast.
When His parents left to go home,
The boy Jesus stayed behind.
Spending time in the Temple,
Maybe picking a wise man's mind.
He was asking many questions
And answering quite a few.
The scholars were very impressed
At the knowledge of this young Jew.
As He sat in the midst of them
They were astonished and amazed,
That this lad was so learn-ed
And they heaped on a lot of praise.
His parents came back and found Him
And when they began to scold.
He said, I'm about my Father's business,
So they put their gripes on hold.
Now Jesus increased in wisdom
And in stature throughout the land
And also found great favor,
In the eyes of God, and man.

1 Corinthians 1:24b
Christ the power of God,
and the wisdom of God.

Nicodemus

There was a man of the Pharisees,
Who was a ruler of the Jews.
He came to Jesus by night
To hear this man's views.
He had heard this man of God
Was doing miracles none other could do.
He was amazed at the things He did
And at His spoken words so true.
Nicodemus heard Jesus say,
Unless a man be born again
He can't enter the Kingdom of God.
There's no way he can get in.
That which is born of flesh, is flesh,
And that born of the spirit, is spirit.
The wind blows where it wants
You cannot see it but you can hear it.
You cannot go back into the womb,
A second time, whether young or old.
You must be born of the spirit.
That is what this man was told.
Nicodemus then said to Christ,
How can these things be?
Please take the time, O Lord,
To explain these things to me.
This is what Nicodemus heard:
We speak of things we know,
But you don't receive our witness,
That is why you fail to grow.

If we tell you of things of the earth
And those you don't believe,
When you are told of heavenly things,
Neither those will you receive.
No man has ascended to Heaven,
Only He that has come down.
It is only through the Son of God,
That you can be Heaven bound.

Blind Bartimaeus

As Jesus went out to Jericho
With His disciples so devout,
A blind man heard it was Jesus
And he began to cry out,
Saying, Jesus, Thou Son of David,
Please have mercy on me.
When the people tried to hush him,
Even louder became his plea.
This man believed in Jesus
And knew He was for real.
When Jesus heard his cry
He stood there very still.
He had Bartimaeus brought to Him
And would now do what was right.
When He asked him what he wanted,
Bartimaeus said, Please restore my sight.
Jesus told him to go his way
For his faith had made him whole.
He immediately received his sight
For believing and for being so bold.

Though I speak with tongues
And have not charity
I am like a tinkling cymbal.
Paul said this with clarity.
Though I prophesy
And understand mysteries,
Yet, still not have love,
God will not be pleased.
Though I bestow my goods,
Helping to feed the poor,
Without love it profits nothing,
Of this I am so sure.
Love is long-suffering,
And is good and kind,
And doesn't behave unseemly,
Just keep that in your mind.
Love is not easily provoked
And does not seek it own.
It does not rejoice in iniquity
But lets the truth be known.
Love bears, hopes and believes,
And endures all things each day.
Love also never fails
Though other things pass away.
Now faith, hope and love abide
But the greatest of these three,
Is not faith, and not hope,
But love, which is charity.

David and Jonathan

King Saul tried to kill David
For the people loved David more than he,
Because David had won many battles
And had kept these people free.

Now the king's son Jonathan
Really did love his dad
But he also loved David,
The best friend he ever had.

He spoke to his father about David,
Saying, it's a bad thing you do,
You should leave him alone,
For he's done nothing to you.

He put his life in his hands
When he fought that Philistine,
And he did it for you and God,
Because he loves you both, O king.

Saul took Jonathan's advice
And would now let David live.
He took him back into his house
And many blessings to him did give.

Then another war broke out
And many thousands David killed.
The people gave him all the glory
And King Saul was not so thrilled.

As David sat in the king's house,
An evil spirit came upon Saul,
Who picked up his javelin
And tried to smite David to the wall.

David managed to get away
And escaped into the night,
But Saul's soldiers came after him
And David had to get out of sight.

He went out through a window
And lowered himself on a rope,
Knowing that if he got caught
There would surely be no hope.

The soldiers again chased David
But failed to bring him back,
So the angry king decided
He would use a different tact.

He told Jonathan he had repented,
But David doubted this was true
And wouldn't go back to the castle
Until for sure he knew.

He and Jonathan soon found out
For David missed a special meal
And the king became so angry,
His own son he tried to kill.

Saul thought Jonathan was rebellious
And favored David, the son of Jesse,
So he hurled his spear at him,
This son he found so pesky.

Jonathan hurried back to David
Telling him what his father had done,
And he and David wept together
For these two were just like one.

They made a vow to each other,
That there would always be peace,
Between them as long as they lived.
It was a vow they would never breach!

Teaching in the church at Antioch
Were Barnabas and Paul,
When the Holy Ghost set them apart
For the work to which they'd been called.
After they fasted and prayed
They left and went on their way,
To Cyprus and other cities
And to another port to stay.
A false prophet lived there
Who desired to hear God's Word.
He wanted to know more about Jesus,
This man of whom he had heard.
Now another prophet in that place
Was standing there also
Trying to keep him from hearing,
Not wanting him to know.
So Paul set his eyes on that prophet,
And being filled with the Holy Ghost,
Said, Child of the devil,
You are one of Satan's host.
Paul then made that man blind
And it was for a very good reason,
For he had spread false doctrines,
So he would not see for a season.
The first prophet was astonished
At this miracle Paul had done.
He would now preach about Jesus
And false doctrines he would shun.

While waiting there in Athens
Paul stood on Mars Hill
And said, you're too religious
And your faith is just for nil.

Somewhere out there is an altar
That I have just been shown,
With certain words inscribed,
Which said to a god unknown.

But now I declare to you
These words of great worth,
I worship the only true God
Who made the heavens and earth.

He dwells in the heavens above,
And not in temples made with hands.
He is loving and mighty
And rules over all the lands.

He is not some graven image
Made of silver, stone or gold.
He is the Lord Almighty
And has vast riches untold.

As Paul talked about Jesus,
The people around him flocked
And a few of them believed
But most of them just mocked.

He preached of how Jesus died
And then rose out of the earth,
And if men believed in Him
They would have a second birth.

Paul knew that to most of these
His words would sound insane,
But to those who would believe,
Someday with Christ, they'd reign!

Love

Now love is long-suffering
And also good and kind.
It doesn't cause an ego
Nor a boastful mind.
It does not behave unseemly
And never seeks its own.
It is not easily provoked
And to it evil is not known.
It does not rejoice in iniquity
But in those things so true,
And bears and believes all things
And hope does then ensue.
True love does not envy
But in all things does endure.
Love doesn't think of evil
But of things clean and pure.
Most of all love never fails
But is there day after day.
Prophesy, tongues and knowledge,
Will soon all pass away.
Now abides faith, love and hope,
But the greatest of these is love,
And it should be unconditional
Like that of our God above.

The Sower of the Seed

As a Sower went forth to sow
He was just doing his deed
But some fell by the wayside
And the fowls ate that seed.

Some fell in stony places
And might have grown except,
The amount of dirt in those rocks
Didn't have much depth.

So when the hot sun came up
The seed all withered away,
An although they sprang up quickly
They lasted just one day.

Some seed fell among the thorns
But when they began to grow,
The thorns quickly choked them out
And they died row after row.

Other seed fell on good ground
And brought forth much fruit we're told.
Some thirty, and some sixty,
Yet, some a hundred fold.

His disciples did not understand,
These stories made no sense.
They could not grasp the meaning,
So Christ came to their defense.

He said, when someone hears the Word
And doesn't really perceive,
They forget what they have heard
And therefore, they don't believe.

The seed in the stony places
Is he, who the Word does hear
And it endures for a short while,
Filling a man's heart with cheer.
However there is no root
And when persecutions arise,
This man is easily offended
And the seed within him dies.
The seed among the thorns
Is he who hears the Word spoke,
But the cares and worries of the world
Causes this man to choke.
Now the seed falling on good ground
Is he who hears and understands,
And bears much fruit for the Lord
And is right there in God's plan.

Jesus Calms the Sea

It came to pass on a certain day
Jesus and His disciples went into a ship,
And He told them to launch out,
It would be a very short trip.
He wanted to cross the lake
To get to the other side,
Yet, as they sailed a storm arose
And it became a very rough ride.

Strong winds blew the ship about
And the waves rose very high.
The disciples became fearful
And were afraid they would die.
The ship was filling with water
And might sink in that lake so deep,
So they went and woke up Jesus
Who had fallen fast asleep.
They said, Master we will perish,
So He arose and calmed the wind.
The raging waters also ceased,
Bringing the bad storm to an end.
Where is your faith, Jesus said,
To His disciples standing near.
He had just saved these men
And taken away their fear.
Yet, they wondered at Him
And to one another did say,
What manner of a man is this,
That the winds and waters obey?

Psalms 107

28. *Then they cry unto the Lord in their trouble,
and He brings them out of their distresses.*

29. *He maketh the storm calm, so that the
waves thereof are still.*

The Kingdom of God is likened to
A man who sowed good seed,
But as he slept his enemy came
And sowed among them poison weed.
This was done in the darkness
So the farmer was unaware,
Until the seeds began to grow
And he saw the weeds in there.
He decided to leave them alone
Just as if he did not care
For he knew when the harvest came,
He could tell the wheat from the tare.
Then he would send his reapers
To gather all the tares to burn
And then go gather the wheat.
This was his main concern.
Now he that sowed good seed
Was likened to Christ, God's Son,
And the field was this old world.
The seeds, the children of His Kingdom.
The enemy was the devil,
Who really hates the light
And most of his evil deeds
Are done in the darkness of the night.
The tares are so-called Christians
But Christ they have never known.
They'll be separated from true believers
And Satan will have them for his own.

Elijah

There was a king named Ahaziah
Who was sick upon his bed
But rather than praying to God
He was inquiring of Baal instead.
Now Elijah accosted his messengers
Who went back to the king to tell,
A man of God said he would die.
That he surely would not get well.
The king sent a captain with fifty men
To bring this Godly man to him.
But Elijah called down fire from God,
That burned up all of them.
Another captain with fifty was sent
And again fire consumed them all.
A third captain with his fifty
On his hands and knees did fall,
And said to Elijah, O man of God
Let our lives be precious in thy sight,
And do not call fire upon us
For we want to do what is right.
God told Elijah to go with them
And tell their king face to face
That he would die upon his bed
For he was a total disgrace.
The king died according to God's Word,
That Elijah had just spoken,
Because he was an evil king
And all God's laws had broken.

God later sent Elijah to Bethel
And Elisha went along too.
He was told to stay behind,
But said, I will never leave you.

Elijah went over to Jordan
And again Elisha went along.
He would not leave Elijah
For he thought that would be wrong.

Elijah took his folded cloak
And the waters of the Jordan smote.
The water parted and on dry land,
They walked, and didn't need a boat.

Elijah then said to Elisha,
Ask what I shall do for thee
And Elisha said, I pray to you
Let your spirit come upon me.

Elijah said, It's a hard thing you ask,
But if you see me when I'm taken away,
You will get two portions of my spirit,
It will be just as you say.

But I also want to tell you this,
If you do not see me when I go,
Even though you want my spirit,
God will not let it be so.

As they stood there talking
There appeared a chariot of fire,
With horses of fire pulling it;
This is what it must require.

When it came down to earth
It parted these two asunder.
A whirlwind took Elijah up
And Elisha was left to wonder,

Why God did not let him die
But translated him home this way.
Was it to give us a picture of Christ,
And His resurrection someday?
That's what a Bible scholar I knew,
Said before she passed away.
She was such a Godly woman,
I would never doubt what she did say.
Elisha got two portions of the spirit
For he stood there and did see,
Elijah being taken to Heaven
And this could happen to you and me.
The scriptures teach that some of us
Certainly will not have to die,
But at Christ's second coming
Will meet Him up in the sky.

Josiah the Child King.

Josiah became the king
When he was only eight,
And ruled Israel for thirty one years
And his kingdom was so great.
He did what was right in God's eyes
Walking in the ways of David the king,
Seeking God very early in life,
Trying to please Him in everything.
He destroyed gold idols and images
When he was only twenty years old.
He tore down the altars of Baalim
And God blessed this child so bold.

Joshua sent out two spies
To view the city of Jericho.
They went into a harlot's house
And no one was supposed to know.
But the king got word of this
And sent Rahab a decree,
Tell me where they are
And then turn them over to me.
But Rahab protected these two,
Saying, They came but are gone now.
They left before the gate was shut
And escaped in the dark somehow.
The soldiers went out hunting for them
For they believed it was a fact,
But she had taken them to the roof
And hid them in stalks of flax.
Rahab told the spies she heard
God had given them this land
And she believed that He had,
This is why she took this stand.
God blessed this faithful woman
And when the city of Jericho fell,
He not only saved her and her kin
But gave them a new place to dwell.

The Temptations of Christ

Now Jesus was led by the Spirit
Out into the wilderness
To be tempted of the devil.
This Son of God, no less.

When He had fasted forty days
And also forty nights,
He was now very hungry
For He had eaten not one bite.

That's when Satan came to Him
And this is what he said,
If thou be the Son of God
Turn these stones into bread.

Christ said, It is written,
Man shall not live by bread alone,
But by every word from God's mouth.
(A truth the devil should have known.)

Satan took Him to a high mountain
And in just a moment of time
Showed Him the kingdoms of the world
And said, Worship me and they'll be thine.

Jesus said, Get thee behind me Satan,
(From God's Word He wouldn't swerve.)
Thou shalt worship the Lord thy God
And Him only shalt thy serve.

Satan brought Him to Jerusalem
And sat Him upon a pinnacle.
Again he said to Jesus,
(His voice being somewhat cynical.)

If thou be the Son of God,
Go and cast thyself down.
He said, Christ wouldn't be in danger
For God's angels were all around.
They would be right there with Him,
So He would not be alone
And they would bear Him up,
Lest He dash His foot against a stone.
Jesus answered and said,
Thou shalt not tempt the Lord thy God,
Then the devil ended his temptations,
And no longer did he prod.
Finally, the devil left Him.
For he was in total defeat,
By the mighty Word of God
Which Jesus did boldly repeat.
Now when we are daily tempted
By the one who tempted our Lord,
We must fight him with the scriptures
Which is our two edged sword.

Hebrews 4:15

*For we have not an high priest which cannot be touched
with the feelings of our infirmities; but was in all points
tempted like we are, yet without sin.*

A Syrian captain named Naaman,
Was a great warrior with Leprosy.
He was told to go down to Israel,
A great man of God to see.
Now Elisha was the prophet
That Naaman was to meet,
So he drove there in his chariot,
But Elisha was not discreet.
He, himself, didn't meet him
But sent his servant to tell,
Naaman to wash in the river
Seven times and he would get well.
His flesh would come back again
For the water would make him clean.
But Naaman was angry now
For he felt he had been demeaned.
Elisha had sent a servant
Instead of meeting him, face to face
And to this great man of valor,
This was a terrible disgrace.
He was not going to wash in the Jordan
But his servants began to prod,
Saying, Master, do as he says
For he is a true man of God.
So Naaman got in the river
And bathed seven times, then smiled,
For when he came out of the water
His skin was like that of a child.
He now believed in Elisha's God
Who ruled over all Israel.
He would now worship this God
And no longer worship Baal.

The Rich Fool

The ground of a certain rich man
Brought forth plentiful crops
But this man had a problem
His barns were filled to their tops.
This man thought to himself
What now must I do?
There's no place to store my fruits.
I'll just build a bigger barn or two.
Once the crops were all stored.
He would then tell his soul
He had enough goods for many years.
This was his main goal.
He would eat, drink and be merry,
And would put himself at ease
But what he didn't know was,
God was very displeased.
The Lord said, O thou fool,
Tonight, thy soul I'll take from thee
And all that thou has stored up,
Then whose shall those things be?
A man who lays up treasure on earth
And is not rich toward God,
Should take no thought of his life.
Now to us that might seem odd.
The body is more than raiment
And life more than just meat.
The ravens do not sow or reap
Yet, God gives them plenty to eat.
So you yourselves should not seek
What you will eat or drink.
God knows you have need of these things.
He'll provide them sooner than you think.

There was a man named Lazzarus
Who was very, very sick.
Jesus really loved this man
So He was told to come real quick.

This sickness was not unto death
But was for God's own glory,
That His Son might be glorified,
That's the truth of this story.

Jesus loved Lazzarus' sisters too
But seemed to be in no hurry
For He tarried three whole days,
Causing Martha and Mary to worry.

Finally, He and His disciples,
Left and went down to Judea,
Though the disciples had some doubts
And maybe just a little fear.

Jesus told them Lazzarus was asleep,
But they didn't understand,
That Jesus meant he was already dead.
This was in His great plan.

Martha went out to meet Jesus,
Knowing if He had been at his side,
Even though Lazzarus was sick,
He would surely not have died.

Jesus said, Your brother shall rise again
But poor Martha was filled with strife
And thought He meant at the resurrection.
He said, I am the resurrection and the life.

Jesus saw Mary and the Jews weeping
And said, Where have you laid him?
They told Him to come and see
And He went along with them.
They knew Jesus loved him very much
Because now Jesus also wept
And groaned within Himself
While standing where Lazzarus slept.
He told them to remove the stone
But they didn't know what to think
For Lazzarus had been dead four days
So they knew his body would stink.
Yet, when the stone was taken away
There was no stench, and they were relieved.
Then Jesus thanked God out loud
So all these people would believe.
Jesus called for Lazzarus,
To come forth out of the cave.
If He hadn't called Lazzarus by name
Others might have come out of their grave.
Lazzarus was bound hand and foot,
Wrapped up from head to toe.
Jesus told them to unwrap him
And they did so and let him go.
Jesus did this great miracle
So many Jews would believe,
That He was truly sent by God
And that they were not deceived.
Now Lazzarus, who was very dead
Just a few moments before,
Was now as alive as any of them.
They wouldn't doubt Jesus anymore.

Armor of God

In order to be strong in the Lord
And in the power of His might
You must put on the whole armor of God
So the wiles of Satan you can fight.
You don't wrestle against flesh and blood
But against the powers of this world.
Against spiritual wickedness on this earth,
Enough to make your hair curl.
You must wear all God's armor
Each and every blessed day
To be able to withstand the evil
That the devil sends your way.
You need to take a firm stand
With God's truth girding your loins
And wear the breastplate of righteousness
That reaches down to your groins.
Put on your feet the Gospel of peace,
As upon this earth you trod,
To help you make it through the day
Winning each battle for God.
You must also put on the shield of faith
That will stop Satan's firey darts
And the helmet of Salvation,
Then God will do His part.
Strap on the sword of the Spirit
Which is the Word of God
And which is much more powerful
Than either steel sword, or rod.

You must always be in prayer
And always on the alert,
That God may give you the boldness,
His mighty Gospel to assert.
Now that you are fully dressed
In the armor of God's army,
No matter what Satan throws at you,
You'll say, Nothing you do can harm me!

Deceivers

Many deceivers are in this world
Who deny Christ has come in the flesh.
They are really a type of antichrist
And with them, you must not mesh.
If anyone comes to witness to you
Who in Christ do not believe,
Do not invite them into your house,
Do not those people receive.
They do not speak the truth,
So don't even wish them Godspeed,
For if you were to do so,
You'd be a part of their evil deeds.

God appeared to Abraham
In the plains of Mamre,
As he sat in the door of his tent
On a hot and sultry day.
He lifted up his eyes and looked
And lo, three men stood there.
He ran out to meet them,
His hospitality with them to share.
Abraham then said, My Lord,
If I have found favor in thy sight
Rest yourselves under the tree
Out of this sun so bright.
He quickly fetched some water
Which he used to wash their feet,
While Sarah was busy making bread
For these three men to eat.
The men got up to leave
Once their meal was done,
And God would return this favor
By giving Abraham a son.
The men looked toward Sodom,
The city God would destroy,
But Abraham thought of the righteous
And was not being very coy.
He said, Lord if there be fifty
Righteous people in that city,
Would you withhold your hand
And upon them take pity?

The Lord agreed that He would.
Abraham said, If there be forty-five
Would you again hold back your wrath
And keep those people all alive?
Again, the Lord said, Yes.
Abraham said, What if there were twenty.
God said, They would be spared,
Even those few would be plenty.
He asked God not to be angry,
Yet, one more time he spake,
Saying, What if you find only ten
Would you spare Sodom for their sake?
Now we know how this story ended
And it truly was a shame,
God couldn't find ten in that city
Who were righteous, and without blame.
We also know about the angels
And how men from each quarter,
Lusted after these two males,
Even refusing to take Lot's daughter.
Yes, God destroyed that vile city
And the destruction was so dire
That Abraham being very far off
Still saw the smoke from that great fire.
Our country has been blessed by God.
It seems our nation He did anoint,
But if we continue in our sinful ways,
We'll soon be like Sodom at some point.

The Christian's duty is very clear
As shown in the writings of Paul.
Our bodies are to be a living sacrifice
Holy and acceptable to God and all.
We must not conform to this world
But with a renewing of the mind
Prove that perfect will of God,
Which is acceptable, good and kind.
We each have a different gift
Given to us by God's grace
And each must determine what that gift is,
Then use it in the right place.
The body of Christ is made up of those
Who prophesy, minister and teach.
Of those who are cheerful givers.
Who show mercy, exhort, and preach.
We must bless those that prosecute us
And weep with those that weep.
We must not do evil for evil
But always the peace must keep.
Vengeance is mine, Says the Lord.
That is what the scriptures say.
We're not to try to avenge ourselves,
For that is not God's way.
If your enemy is hungry, feed him.
Give him both drink and bread,
For in so doing you will heap,
Coals of fire upon his head.
If all those things written above
Have been read and understood.
You will not fight evil with evil
But overcome evil with good!

Jairus' Daughter

Behold a man named Jairus
Came and fell at Jesus' feet.
He had only one daughter
Who was young and sweet
But she was now very sick,
And at home in her bed lying.
He wanted Jesus to come right away
To keep his child from dying.
Jesus was detained somewhat
For people swamped Him like a flood.
A woman touched His robe
And was healed of an issue of blood.
When she saw that Jesus knew,
She came before Him and fell down.
She told Him she had been healed
And told others standing around.
Now as Jesus spoke to this woman
There came one who told Jairus,
His daughter was already dead,
So there was no need to trouble Jesus.
Then Jesus told Jairus not to fear,
Just believe, and she'll be whole.
This was hard for him to do
But he believed as he was told.

When they got to the house
Where Jairus' daughter had died,
Jesus let only Peter, James and John
And her mother and father inside.
Everyone wept and wailed
But Jesus standing by her bed,
Told them she was just asleep,
That their daughter was not dead.
They all laughed at Him
For she was as dead as she could be,
But Jesus then spoke a word or two
And alive again, became she.
Her spirit had come to her once more
And she got up right away.
It was just one more miracle
That Jesus had done that day.
Her parents were very astonished,
Yet, Jesus did charge them
To tell no one what was done
And they listened, and obeyed Him.
When Christ tells us something to do
Though we might not understand,
If we will just trust in Him
We'll be safely in His hands.

The Romans Road

Some scriptures tell us how to be saved:
The Romans Road is how they're known.
They are given to us in simple terms
So we can't say we've not been shown.
First, there is *Romans 3:10*
There is none righteous, no not one.
Followed by *Romans 3:23*
All short of God's glory have come.
Next *Romans 5:12* lets us know
By one man sin entered in
And death passed to all men
Because now they all have sinned.
Go now to *Romans 6:23* where
The wages of sin is death we're told,
But the gift of God is eternal life
Which though Jesus Christ unfolds.
Now back to *Romans 5:8*
That while we were yet sinners
Christ commended His love toward us,
And died for us, making us winners.
Flip now to *Romans 10:9*
Which tells us what we must do
In order to have eternal life,
And that God will follow through.
Then comes *Romans 10:13*
That says whosoever calls on His name
Will be saved by the blood of Jesus
And will never again be the same.
Dear friend if you'll travel this road
And believe it deep within your heart.
You'll belong to God for eternity
And from you He will never depart!

Now once a person has been saved
By accepting Jesus Christ
And believe He died for his sin
And on Calvary paid the price.
That person is truly born again
And now has a nature that's new
And as far Salvation goes,
There's nothing more he can do.
That old saying is really true,
Once saved, always saved,
Because the road to Heaven
With Jesus' blood was paved.
And all throughout the Bible,
There are promises God made
That we won't lose our Salvation,
That it will never leave, nor fade.
You need to find a promise verse
And ingrain it in your heart,
For example Romans ten thirteen,
That says God will do His part.
Now Satan will do all he can
To make you doubt, and steal your joy,
But with your chosen promise verse
You can defeat his every ploy.
When he tempts you, and he will,
Just quote your verse, even shout it!
It proves to him you belong to God,
And you have no doubt about it!

Christian Cruises

If you've never been on a cruise
With IN TOUCH MINISTRIES®
You've missed a little bit of Heaven
While cruising out on the seas.
You'll be there with Dr Stanley
The well-known preacher on TV
And Bob Schipper and other preachers
Who teach the scriptures easily.
These pastors preach the Gospel.
Christian entertainers play and sing.
The fellowship with other Christians
Is really a bless-ed thing.
Stan Whitmire's music is uplifting,
As he plays that piano, oh so grand.
The Specks' and Greater Vision's singing
Gives more joy than one can stand.
Dennis Swanberg's standup comedy
And Geraldine's ventriloquism,
Really light up these cruises
Like sunbeams on a prism.
But Geraldine's dummy, Ricky,
Victimizes the preachers and singers
And when he says, I love you,
He always follows with a stinger.
Now if you'll remember that Ricky
Is made partly out of wood.
The poem on the next page
Will be more easily understood.

You had better not get on the stage
With Geraldine and Ricky.
Now Geraldine is not so bad
But her dummy is very tricky.
He looks so young and innocent
Dressed in his fancy "get up,"
But when he asks a question
You know that you've been "set up."
You cannot get the best of him
No matter how hard you try.
He'll find a way to embarrass you
Even if he has to lie.
Wow! He treats Dr. Stanley bad
And makes his face turn red.
Imagine what he would do to you;
I think enough's been said.
There is a way to stop Ricky
And also give him quite a fright.
Just tell him you have a pocketful,
Of hungry....live....**Termites**!

(On a recent cruise to the Bahamas, Geraldine and her dummy Ricky were
entertainers, and I watched this little guy really trash everyone he had on
stage with him, always getting the best of them. I wrote this poem about
Ricky, and my wife liked it so much she asked me to do it in the Talent Show
that night instead of "Jonah and the Whale." It went over great! I think even
the little dummy liked it.)

Barnabas and the other believers
Were all of one heart and soul,
So they sold their land and houses
And no money did they withhold.
They brought it all to the apostles
Who blessed their unselfish deeds,
And then distributed the money
To each man according to his needs.
But Ananias and Sapphira,
Who evidently didn't think twice,
Conspired to sell a possession
And keep part of its selling price.
Ananias brought what was left
And laid it at the Apostle's feet
Not knowing Peter already knew
That he was a liar and a cheat.
Peter asked him why they let Satan,
Cause them to lie to the Holy Ghost
And not give Him all the money
But keep back some, if not most?
As soon as Ananias heard this
He dropped dead then and there
And great fear came upon the people.
This was hard for them to bear.

Ananias was taken and buried
And hours later, his wife came in.
She didn't know that her husband
Was struck dead because of their sin.
Peter then asked Sapphira
If they had sold houses, land and such
And she answered him with lies,
Saying, We sold them for so much.
She too, then dropped dead
For she also was filled with greed,
And she gave up the ghost
Due to her most evil deed.
Now God loves a cheerful giver,
One who gives with a willing heart.
Not like Ananias and Sapphira,
Who were not being very smart.
When God lays it on your heart
To give Him a certain sum,
Don't do like those two did
Because that would be real dumb!

2 Corinthians 9:7

> *Every man according as he purposes in his heart, so let him give;*
> *not grudgingly, or of necessity: for God loves a cheerful giver.*

There was a man of Caesarea
From the tribe called the Italian band.
He was a centurion named Cornelius,
A very good and devout man.
He gave much alms to the poor
And prayed to God always.
He had a vision about the ninth hour,
Of an angel coming to say,
You must send some men to Joppa,
Not many, just one or two,
And have them find a man called Peter
Who can tell you what you should do.
After the angel told Cornelius this,
He was finished and he departed.
Cornelius then got two of his men
To pack up so they could get started.
When they left on their journey,
They traveled hard and as they drew nigh,
Peter went up on the housetop to pray
And became hungry by and by.
He would have eaten right then,
But we know it wasn't by chance
That while the food was being prepared
He fell into a very deep trance.
In a vision he saw Heaven opened
And a vessel coming down to him.
It was like a great white sheet
With four corners that were so trim.

Inside were four-footed beasts
And creeping things, and fowls of the air.
An angel told Peter to kill and eat,
But poor Peter just did not dare.
He told the Lord he had never eaten
Anything common or unclean.
The voice told Peter a second time
Don't call common what God has cleaned.
The sheet was lowered and raised three times
And as Peter pondered what it meant,
The Holy Spirit told him
About the men Cornelius had sent.
These men found Simon's house
And now stood before his gate
And were calling out to Peter.
Now isn't God's timing great?
Peter came down to meet these men,
And said, I am he whom you seek.
He asked them why they had come
And their answer was so unique.
They said, An angel told their Master
To send for Peter so he could share,
The things God commanded of him
With the Gentiles waiting back there.
Peter told them it was unlawful
For a man who was a Jew
To keep company with Gentiles,
But God showed him what he must do.

He must never call any man common
For God is no respecter of men.
He must tell all men about Jesus
And how He died for their sin.
While Peter was telling about Christ,
The Holy Ghost fell on them
And each Gentile then believed
And the Spirit entered into him.
Peter asked if anyone would forbid
That these Gentiles be baptized
And not a single man spoke up,
Much to everyone's surprise.
But Peter had to answer questions,
For his people back in Judea,
So he explained the situation
And they agreed or so it appears,
Because they held their peace
And glorified God, and did say,
God granted repentance to the Gentiles.
They have become one of us this day.
God is no respecter of persons,
Whether they be rich or poor,
Or of a different nationality,
They can get into Heaven for sure.
But there is one big requirement
For the gates to open and let them in,
They must believe in Jesus Christ
And believe He died for all their sin.

Ten Commandments

God gave us these commandments:

1. You shall have no gods before me.

2. You shall not make graven images,
   (or bow down to them on your knee.)

3. You shall not take the Lord's name in vain

4. Remember to keep holy the Sabbath day.
   (six days we are to work,
   and rest on the seventh, that's God's way.)

5. You must honor your father and mother.

6. And you surely shall not kill.

7. You shall not commit adultery.

8. And you shall not steal.

9. You shall not bear false witness
   (at any time) against your neighbor.

10. You shall not covet your neighbor's possessions.
    (If you do you'll lose God's favor.)

Those are God's commandments
Which He has put in place
And no man can ever keep them
Except through God's loving grace.
That's why God bestowed His grace on us
When He put Jesus on the cross,
Letting Him die there for our sin,
To save us from being lost.
Since man couldn't keep these laws,
God prepared a sacrifice,
His only Son whom He loved,
Had to pay that awesome price.

Now some Christians may not agree
With the poem "No doubt about it.»
But there can be no peace inside
If you try to live without it.

I once believed that same way
But God showed me I was wrong
And now there's peace within my heart
All day and all night long.

God put Jesus on that cross
With a sinner on either side,
More than two thousand years ago
To save my worthless hide.

He hung there and took the blame
For my sins before I was born,
With nails piercing both His hands,
And wearing that crown of thorns.

His precious blood covered **all** my sins,
Not just those committed today,
But all those done, or that will be done,
Past, present and always.

For, by grace, I am saved through faith
And that not of myself.
It is truly a gift from God.
Yes, straight from Christ Himself.

One cannot live a life good enough
For his good to outweigh the bad.
Yet, many people believe this
And that makes me very sad,

For they don't know if they are saved
From one day until the next,
And the uncertainty of all that
Must keep their hearts perplexed.
O the joy and peace they'd have
Each night as they went to bed,
If they believed for **all** their sins,
Not just today's, was His blood shed.
I know from experience
The comfort and joy it brings,
Knowing He did it just for me
Without attaching any strings.

Jude 1:1. Jude, the servant of Jesus Christ and brother of James, to them that are **sanctified [saved]** *by God the Father, and* **preserved** *in Jesus Christ, and called:*

Samson

The Philistines ruled over Israel
And God sought a reason at that time
To have Samson do battle for Him.
Samson was now just in his prime.
So God let him see this woman,
Whom he wanted for his wife
But since she was a Philistine,
His parents were filled with strife.
Yet, they went along with Samson
Down to the valley of Timnath,
Where along the way a young lion,
Stood and roared in Samson's path.

The Spirit came mightily on Samson
And he ripped the lion apart,
Using only his two bare hands
And doing it with much heart.
He finally met this woman
Who pleased him so very well.
He would come back later and take her,
To the land where they would dwell.
Going back home he saw bees and honey
In the carcass of the lion.
He ate some, and took some home,
For both his parents to dine on.
There was a tradition in that day
Young grooms would give a feast.
They would kill a fatted calf or lamb,
Or some other tasty beast.
That's when Samson posed a riddle
About the lion and the honey sweet.
He would pay the men who solved it
With thirty garments and thirty sheets.
If they didn't solve it in thirty days
They'd have to pay him the same.
They made his wife give them the answer,
Then straight to Samson they came,
And said, What's sweeter than honey,
And much stronger than a lion.
They didn't know but their answer,
Was one many men would die on,
Because Samson killed thirty men
And gave their garments to all those
Who had cheated and solved his riddle.
These were their promised sheets and clothes.

Samson then decided to visit his wife
And took a goat to her father's house.
But she had been given to his friend
And was no longer his spouse.

His father-in-law thought he hated her
And had given his daughter away
And Samson became so angry
He burnt fields of corn that day.

He caught three hundred foxes,
Then tied torches to their tails
And turned them loose in the fields.
A tactic that did not fail.

The Philistines killed his wife and her father,
Their anger against him to appease.
Samson decided to avenge his wife
And after that his fighting would cease.

Therefore, he killed many Philistines,
And it was such a senseless slaughter,
But he did it for his dead wife
Who was the Timnites daughter.

Three thousand of Samson's people came,
Saying, The Philistines were harming them.
Because Samson had killed their people,
For what they had done to him.

He went with them to his enemies,
But first he made them swear,
They themselves wouldn't harm him
But would deliver him safely there.

They promised, and bound him tightly,
And brought him out of the rocks.
When the Philistines saw him they shouted
But Samson gave them quite a shock.

The Spirit of the Lord came on him
And he tore the ropes off his hands
And with jawbone of a donkey
Killed a thousand men in that land.
Yes, Samson was a mighty warrior,
Whom God sometimes had to nudge.
He judged Israel for twenty years,
So he was also a mighty Judge.
Samson then went down to Lehi
And was so thirsty, to God he cried,
You delivered me from the Philistines
Are you now going to let me die?
God caused a crack in the ground
And water came out and he drank.
His spirit returned and he was revived
And I'm sure he gave God thanks.
He then went to a city called Gaza,
Not seeming to have a care
But his enemies surrounded the city,
When told that Samson was there.
They waited in darkness at the gate.
Planning to kill him at daylight
But Samson laid low for some time
Then got up and quickly took flight.
He grabbed the doors of the gate,
Along with the strong gate posts
And pulled them out of the ground,
Thereby eluding his angry host.
God used Samson's great strength
To help make His plan unfold,
And He will do the same with us,
If we'll just do as we are told.

Job

There was a man in the city of Uz
Who was perfect in God's sight.
He hated evil and loved God
And was righteous and upright.
He had three pretty daughters
And seven handsome sons
And offered burnt offerings for them,
In case there was sin in anyone.
Job was a man of great substance,
The richest man in the East,
Whose family got together often
And always had a great feast.
He had three thousand camels
And seven thousand sheep in his fold.
Five hundred oxen and donkeys
And a very large household.
Satan walked to and fro on the earth
Causing havoc and discord.
One day he came to God
And stood there before the Lord.
He was always seeking someone new
Whose character he could disrobe,
So God put this question to him
Have you considered my servant Job?
Satan said, You have built a hedge,
Protecting Job on all sides.
You have blessed the work of his hands
And blessed the land where he resides.

Satan told God Job would curse Him
If things were different from this,
So God gave him the power
To cause Job's blessings to go amiss.
First, a messenger came to Job
And told him, while maybe bowing,
His oxen and donkeys had been stolen
And some servants killed while plowing.
While this man was still speaking,
A second servant came and said.
Lightning had burnt up all his sheep
And struck more servants dead.
Before this servant was finished
A third man came with a story true.
The enemy had taken his camels
And killed more servants too.
As he was speaking a fourth man came
Telling him of a great, strong wind
That had blown his son's house down,
Killing his children, yes all ten.
Job arose and tore off his clothes,
Shaved his head, and fell to the ground
And began worshipping God.
Not cursing Him, or making evil sounds.
Job said, Naked I came into the world
And naked I will return,
The Lord gives and He takes away.
This is what Job had learned.

Job continued to worship God
And in all his troubles did not sin.
So Satan came to God once more
And God said, Consider Job again.
There is none like him in the earth
For he has held fast his integrity
And despite all that you did to him,
He never once cursed Me.
Satan then told the Lord,
If it had been Job's own skin
It would be a different story
And Job would curse Him in the end.
God again put Job in Satan's hands
But would not let him take his life.
He could do anything else he wanted,
To cause him misery and strife.
The devil went forth from the Lord
And caused Job to have boils so sore.
His body was covered from head to foot
And Satan kept on adding more.
Job sat in pain in the ashes
And his sores with pottery scraped.
The cursing of God Satan predicted,
Just never did take shape.
Now Job's wife came to him,
Saying, Just curse God and die!
But Job called her a foolish woman
And he wasn't telling a lie.

He asked her how they could accept
All the good things from God's hands
And not also accept the bad things?
But she just did not understand.
Neither did his three close friends
Who came to mourn with him for days,
But instead of comforting him
They began to question his ways.
These three friends all believed,
That Job had committed a sin
And if he would confess and repent,
God would bless this man again.
Now Job went into much discourse,
Answering the questions of each man
Because they still doubted his motives
And wanted him to change his stand.
Job knew that he had not sinned
But to his God whom he did trust,
Confessed that he hated himself
And repented in ashes and dust.
God then spoke to Job's friends,
Who knew they had made God mad,
For not speaking of Him rightly
As their good friend Job had.
They had to give some beasts to Job
And offer burnt offerings too.
God told them once they did that,
Job will pray for each of you.

These men did as they were told
And did nothing underhanded
And God restored Job's family,
Because they did as He commanded.
He would now increase Job's substance.
Doubling everything he ever had.
How good this must have made Job feel,
After such a long time of feeling bad.
Job now had six thousand camels
And fourteen thousand sheep.
One thousand oxen and donkeys,
Which all were his to keep.
God even gave him seven sons
An three very beautiful daughters,
Because he never once cursed God.
Though his wife really thought he "oughta."
This should be a good lesson for us,
We too should remain strong and bold
And trust God through all our troubles,
Knowing that He's in full control.

1 Peter 1:9

Be sober, be vigilant; because your adversary
the devil, as a roaring lion, walks about,
seeking whom he may devour.

It happened one day that Jonathan,
The much loved son of Saul,
Went to the Philistine's camp
And didn't tell his father at all.
Saul was sitting outside the city
Under a big pomegranate tree,
And had six hundred men with him.
Jonathan had only his man, and he.
These two went out of their camp
And no one knew they were gone.
Saul would have surely stopped him
If somehow he had known.
Jonathan knew where he was going
So he didn't need a guide.
He chose a pass to go through
That had sharp rocks on either side.
He was sure the Lord was with him
Even though they were only two
And knew God could win any battle
With many men or just a few.
Now Jonathan's armor bearer
Was with him from the start
And always encouraged him
Just to follow his own heart.
Jonathan said, Let's show ourselves
To those Philistines over there
And if they say, We'll come to you,
We'll stay here and our lives we'll spare.

But if they tell us to come to them,
It will surely be God's sign
That He has given them to me
And everything will be just fine.
Jonathan and his man stood up
And climbed out of the rocks.
The enemy said, Come to us,
But they were in for quite a shock.
They thought there were more soldiers
Hiding among those stones.
They didn't know that Jonathan
And his man were all alone.
So God gave the enemy to Jonathan
And as they fell down before him
His armor bearer took his sword
And killed each one of them.
In this, his very first battle,
Jonathan slew about twenty men,
Because the Lord was there with him
And stayed with him until the end.
This lad had faith like David had,
When he killed Goliath the Philistine,
Which was so great a victory,
Such as men had never seen.
Now God can use each one of us
Just like He did this lad,
If we will only have great faith
Like he and David had!

Ten Virgins

Ten virgins took their lamps
And went to meet the bridegroom.
Five of them were very wise
But the foolish five were doomed.
The wise ones filled their lamps
And also took extra oil.
The five foolish didn't bother
For it would have caused them extra toil.
So while the bridegroom tarried
The ten virgins rested and slept.
When the bridegroom came
They all went out to meet him, except,
The five foolish virgins
For their lamps had gone out,
And no one would give them oil
So they were left alone to pout.
While they went to buy some,
The others went in the marriage hut.
The foolish ones came back later
But the door was already shut.
They said, Lord open the door,
But he said, I know you not.
It was like he never knew them
Or maybe like he forgot.
Watch therefore, He said to them
You don't know the day or hour,
When the Son of Man will come,
No man has that power.

We, too, may have good intentions
Like those foolish virgins had,
But miss out on God's blessings
And end up being very sad.
The Kingdom of Heaven is likened to
Those ten wise and foolish virgins,
The doors will be opened to the wise,
But the foolish will not get in.

Five Thousand Fed

When Jesus heard that Herod
Had cut off John the Baptist's head,
He went out to a desert place
Where five thousand would be fed.
When the people heard of this
They followed Him from the city
And when Jesus saw the multitude
He was filled with compassion and pity.
So He proceeded to heal the sick
Until His disciples came to say,
We have no food for them to eat
You must send them all away.
But Jesus told them not to depart
They would be given food to eat.
With only five loaves and two fishes,
This would be quite some feat.

The loaves were brought to Jesus,
Who had the people all sit down,
Then He blessed and broke those loaves
And more food then did abound.
Each of those people ate
Until their stomachs were filled.
And of all the food not eaten
There were a full twelve baskets still.
Five thousand men were fed,
Not counting each woman and child
And since so much was left over,
It must have made them smile.
No one thought this could happen
But it was Christ's miracle that day.
He can still work miracles for us
If we'll just let Him have His way!

Jesus Walks on the Water

After Jesus fed the five thousand,
He had His disciples get on a ship
And go across the lake.
It would be a very short trip.
Then Jesus went up to the mountains,
After sending the people away,
For He needed to be left alone
And have some private time to pray.

But the boat was in choppy waters
And the wind fierce and contrary.
The ship was being tossed about
And the disciples inside were wary.
Jesus walked on the water to them
And they were filled with fear
For they thought He was a ghost,
But He said, It is I, be of good cheer.
Peter answered Him and said,
Lord if it's you, bid me come,
And Christ told him to do so,
Then Peter did something dumb.
He was walking to Jesus on the water
But he took his eyes off of Him
And saw those boisterous waves
And started sinking and could not swim.
He shouted out, Lord save me,
Probably flinging his arms about.
Then Christ said, Thou of little faith,
Because Peter had begun to doubt.
When they got into the boat
Everyone fell and worshipped Him,
Knowing He was the Son of God
And they now were not so grim.
Peter was walking on the water,
But he took his eyes off Christ.
If we don't keep our eyes on Him,
We too will have to pay a price!

Daniel as a Boy

When Daniel was just a boy
Of maybe nine or ten,
He was chosen by the king
To be trained by his men.
He was a captive in Babylon,
This lad of royal descent,
And had to be without blemish,
To be a part of this event.
He had to understand science,
And be very skillful and smart,
Also loyal to his king,
With a wise and trusting heart.
Daniel was taken to the palace
Where for three years he'd serve,
While learning to speak Chaldean,
But this lad had lots of nerve.
He would not drink the wine
When he sat down to eat
And would not defile his body,
By eating any red meat.
The king thought he must do this
To keep his young body strong,
But at the end of three years
Daniel would prove him to be wrong.
He asked the man in charge
To let him prove himself ten days.
Letting him live on bread and water,
Saying, I'll stay healthy in all ways.

Now this man really liked Daniel
But knew his head would be in danger,
For if Daniel didn't stay healthy,
He would feel all the king's anger.
Yet, he followed his own instincts
And withheld the meat and wine,
Hoping at the end of ten days,
Daniel's health would be just fine.
Now at the end of those days,
Daniel was wiser, stronger and more able
To serve his beloved king
Than any man who ate from his table.
Daniel's master then went to the king
And gave him this good report,
That Daniel was one of the lads,
Who would soon serve in his court.
If we are asked to do something
That we know is not of God,
Whether it be in word or deed,
Or putting something into our "bod".
Remember how God blessed Daniel
When he just plainly refused,
To eat meat and sin against God
And how greatly he was used.
If we'll be more like Daniel
And walk daily in God's ways,
Bringing Him honor and glory,
He will bless us all of our days!

The Forgotten Dream

In the second year of his reign
Nebuchadnezzar had a dream.
His spirit was troubled deeply
And he lost much sleep it seems.
He called his magicians to him,
And his astrologers and sorcerers too,
To tell him what his dream meant
But they didn't know what to do.
For when they asked the king
To tell his dream to them
The king couldn't remember it.
It had completely eluded him.
He was very upset with them
And this threat to them, he put,
If they didn't interpret his dream,
Into small pieces they'd be cut.
But, if they gave him the answer,
Which he wanted now, not later,
He'd reward them with many gifts,
And their honor would be greater.
They again asked him for his dream
And once more he refused,
For he couldn't remember it,
So the wise men were all confused.
They told him it was impossible,
That there was not a man on earth
Who could interpret his dream,
Or to explain to him it's worth.

The king didn't trust these men
For their words were somewhat curious
And he became very angry at them,
In fact, he became furious.
He sent an order to his soldiers
To bring every wise man to be slain.
This included Daniel and his friends
Who for the king's service were trained.
Daniel asked the captain of the guards,
Why the king made this decree,
And was told the wise men failed the king,
So it was due to their inability.
Daniel was then granted more time
And he and his companions three,
Got on their knees and asked God
For His great wisdom and mercy.
God revealed the dream to Daniel
Who then praised his God on high
For showing him what the dream meant,
So no one would have to die.
Daniel told the king no man,
Could ever his dream reveal.
Only his God in Heaven could,
Who was alive and very real.
He told him there was an image,
In his dream with a head of gold.
With a breast and arms of silver,
And these other things he told.
It had a belly and thighs of bronze,
With legs and feet of iron and clay.
It was smote into pieces by a stone,
Which a strong wind carried away.

There was no place on earth for them,
Though the pieces were so small.
Yet, the stone that broke the image
Became a mountain great and tall.
The meaning of your dream is
That you are a king of kings,
And God has given you this kingdom
With all the power and glory it brings.
He has made you a great ruler,
You are that head of gold.
You rule all men in this land,
And beasts in the fields and folds.
There will rise a kingdom of silver,
It will be inferior to thee.
Then a third kingdom of bronze,
Which will rule the earth, you see.
A fourth kingdom of iron,
Will be mixed with miry clay
And will be both strong and weak.
This is what God had Daniel say.
In the days of these kingdoms,
God will set up a Kingdom of His own
Which will never be destroyed,
But will be the strongest ever known.
The king then fell before Daniel,
And said, Your God is the Lord of kings,
And He is the God of gods,
Who knows all secret things.
He then made Daniel the ruler
Over all the land of Babylon,
And over the governors and wise men,
Who would obey him from now on.

Daniel asked the king to put Shadrack,
Meshack and Abednego,
Over the affairs of Babylon
And the king agreed to do so.
Because of Daniel's belief in God
His influence on the king was great.
The king therefore honored him
By letting him sit at his gate.
Daniel knew he needed God
And could not have done this on his own.
We, like Daniel, need God everyday,
This is a fact well known!

Land of Milk and Honey

Caleb and Joshua were two spies
Sent by Moses to Canaan.
God was giving it to them,
This great and fruitful land.
They were to observe the people
To see if they were weak or strong.
To see if the land was fat or lean
For it would be theirs before long.
He told them to have courage
And bring back fruits of the land.
So they cut a big cluster of grapes,
That couldn't be carried by one man.
They also got many other fruits,
But mainly pomegranates and figs.
Then they returned after forty days
With their bounty, oh so big.

They told Moses and all their people
About their journey, their pursuit.
Of the goodness of the land,
And then showed them all the fruit.
The land flows with milk and honey,
Is what they told this throng,
And it is full of many riches,
Which will be ours before long.
Now Caleb spoke to the people,
Saying, Let us go right now
And possess this great land,
For God will give it to us somehow.
The other spies who went with him
Did not think this ought to be,
Saying, Those men are too big
And very much stronger than we.
So because of their unbelief,
Which was the reason for their fears,
They would wander in the wilderness
For exactly forty years.
They wouldn't enter the Promised Land,
But both Caleb and Joshua would,
Because these two trusted the Lord
And always for Him they stood.
Many promises are made by God
But in them we must believe
And trust Him for everything,
In order His blessings to receive.

Proverbs 3:5,6

Trust in the Lord with all your heart; lean not to your own understanding. In all ways acknowledge Him, and He will direct your paths.

Forgive us of our sins, Lord.
As we forgive those out there
Who may sin against us,
This should be our prayer.
Jesus gave us this example
When teaching us how to pray
And we should heed His words
And say our prayers His way.
As we look at His words
They tell us what we must do,
And that is to forgive others
So that God will forgive you.
We can't harbor bitterness,
That point is very clear,
And have close fellowship with God,
That we Christians hold so dear.
If we confess our sins each day
God will be faithful and just
To forgive us of those sins,
But please understand we must,
Forgive those who sin against us,
That is where we have to start,
To have a closer walk with God
And be nearer to His heart.
Forgiving those who harm us
Is how God wants us to act,
And if we don't it boils down to,
This plain and simple fact.
If you don't, He won't!

Be quick to listen, yes fast to hear,
Especially with those you love so dear.
Be slow to speak, just hold your tongue,
Think of what you will say before you've begun.
Be slow to anger, don't let wrath slip through,
You're sure to hurt someone if you do.
Lay apart all filth and naughtiness.
Stay in God's Word, and your soul He will bless.

Cain and Abel

We've all heard the story
Of Cain and Abel
And know it is true
And not just a fable.
Don't depend on your works
As did brother Cain
If you do your efforts
Will all be in vain.
But be like Abel
And not undecided
Just take the Lamb
That God has provided.
He will be your Lord
On your journey down here,
And when He's in control
You path will be clear.

The Philippi Jail.

There is an old, old jail in Philippi
Paul was imprisoned there
Because he preached the Gospel
And was so quick to share,
How God did choose a virgin
To bear his only Son,
Who would live a perfect, sinless life,
He would be the only one.
He'd give that perfect, sinless life
On that cross at Calvary,
So each one of God's children,
From their sins could be set free.
Now as we celebrate this day,
This special Christmas morn.
Let's not forget the reason why
This precious child was born.

The Pharisee and the Publican

Two men went into the temple to pray,
And this a truthful fact.
One was a "righteous" Pharisee;
The other, a man who collected tax.
The Pharisee was so full of pride,
Not praying to God at all,
Just making himself feel very good,
And making the publican feel small.
He said he was not like other men,
Extortioners, adulterers, unjust,
Or even as this tax collector,
For in his own works he did trust.
This man fasted twice a week
And gave a tithe of all he possessed
But during his long prayer,
Not one sin did he confess.
The Publican stood far off and said,
God be merciful to me a sinner
And beat his chest and repented.
Who do you think came out a winner?
The Pharisee only praised himself
So by his own words he defaulted.
The publican humbled himself,
So he was justified and exalted.

(After saying her prayers one night, my four year old daughter told her mother it was her turn. My wife told her she had already said her prayers to herself, to which my daughter replied, "Mother! You've got to say them to God.")

Salvation

True Salvation is of God
And seems to come in three parts.
The first part belongs to God,
That is where Salvation starts.
John three sixteen tell us,
God loves us and gave His Son,
By sending Him down from Heaven,
To see that His work was done.
God commended His love toward us,
As it says in Romans five, verse eight,
And while we were yet sinners
Christ did His part and sealed our fate.
He laid down His life for us,
(That is written in John ten),
No man took it from Him
And He took it up again.
We now come to the third part
Of man confessing Christ as Lord
And believing God raised Him up,
As it says in His Holy Word.
Everyone who believes this
And calls on Jesus' name
Will be saved by His shed blood
And will never be the same.
We know God has done part one,
And Jesus has done part two.
If you really want to be saved,
Part three is up to you.

Index:

This title was published by
VICTORY GRAPHICS AND MEDIA
9731 East 54th Street
Tulsa, Oklahoma 74146

For more information on this and other titles available
please contact us at www.victorygraphicsandmedia.com

Additional copies of this book are available online at:
www.biblestoriesinrhyme.com
or at your local bookstore.

For speaking engagements please contact the author at:
770-957-3286 or via e-mail at: geecrum@bellsouth.net

To purchase a copy of *A Little Boy and His Trains*
Please contact Xlibris at 1-888-795-4274 or www.xlibris.com